CW01315526

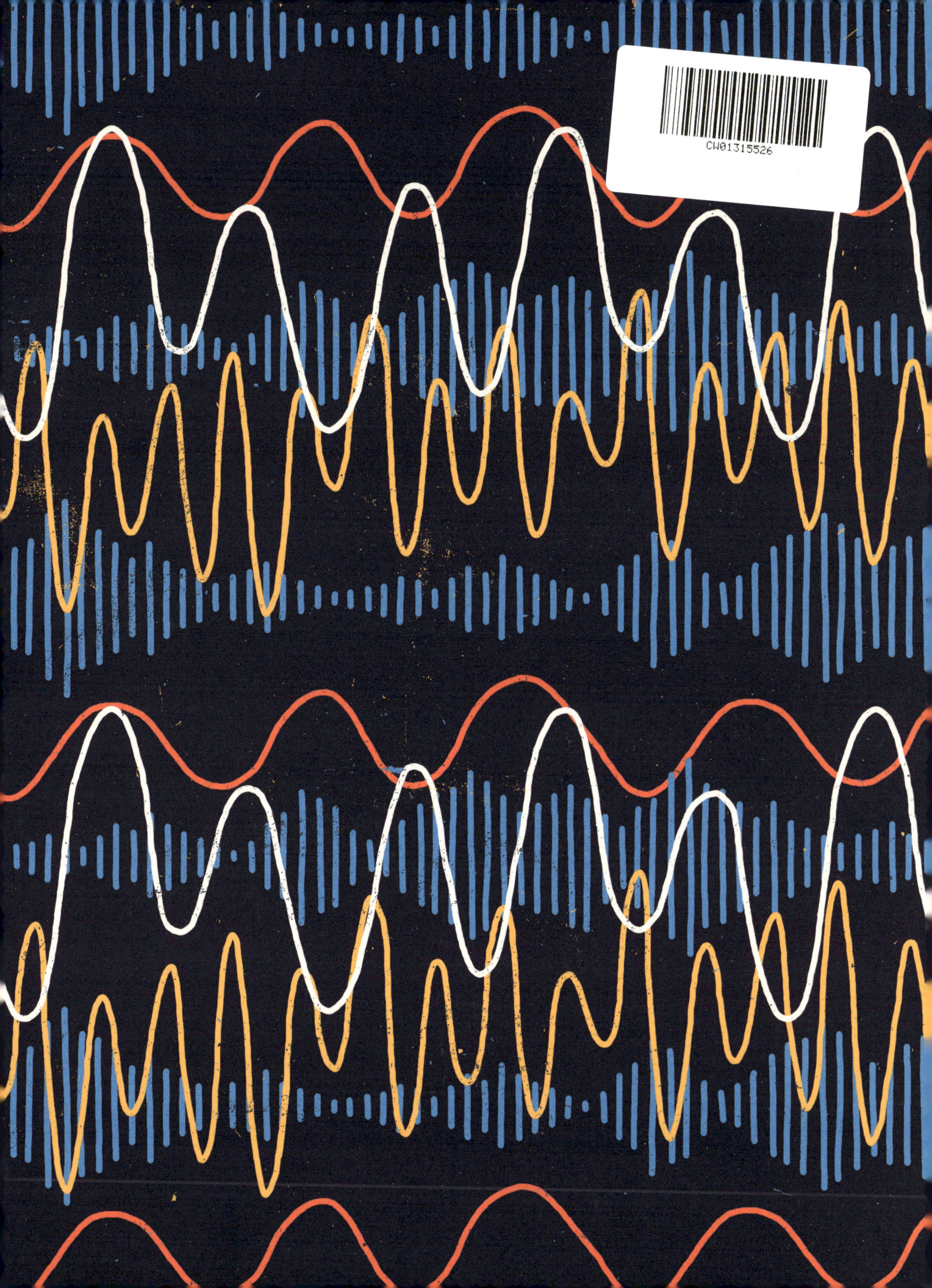

For Andrew, Adrian and their cousins,
in memory of Mark – J.H.

For my parents, who taught me
how to get involved – J.L.

For my family, who have always given me invaluable support,
and for all the people involved in this book, whom I have
had the opportunity to learn so much from – A.D.

A TEMPLAR BOOK

First published in the UK in 2022 by Templar Books,
an imprint of Bonnier Books UK,
4th Floor, Victoria House,
Bloomsbury Square, London WC1B 4DA
Owned by Bonnier Books,
Sveavägen 56, Stockholm, Sweden
www.bonnierbooks.co.uk

Text copyright © 2022 by Joan Haig and Joan Lennon
Illustration copyright © 2022 by André Ducci
Design copyright © 2022 by Templar Books

1 3 5 7 9 10 8 6 4 2

All rights reserved

ISBN 978-1-78741-732-8

This book was typeset in Archer and Tomarik.
The illustrations were created digitally.

Edited by Carly Blake and Lydia Watson
Designed by Adam Allori
Production by Neil Randles

Printed in Latvia

TALKING HISTORY

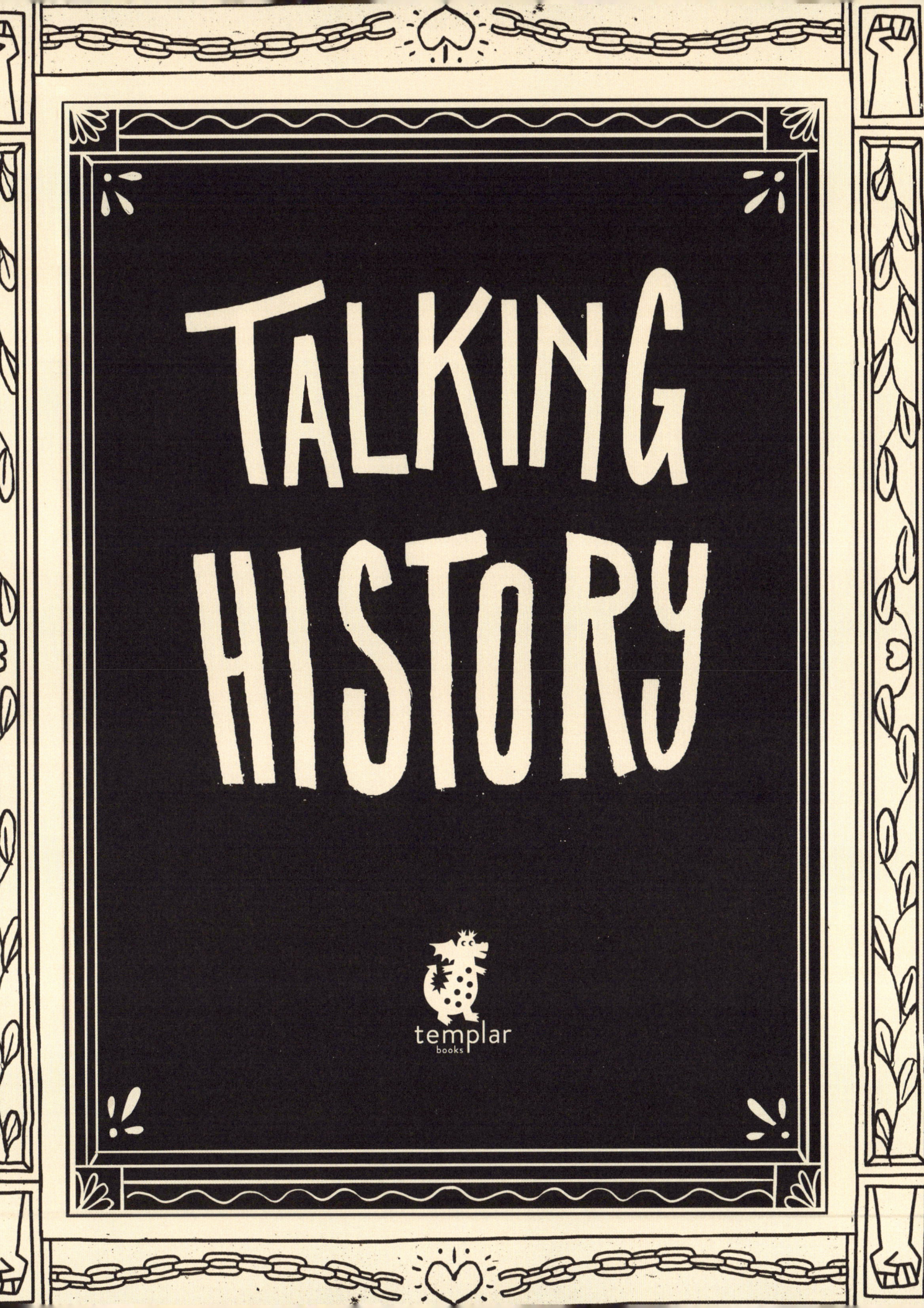

templar
books

FROM THE AUTHORS

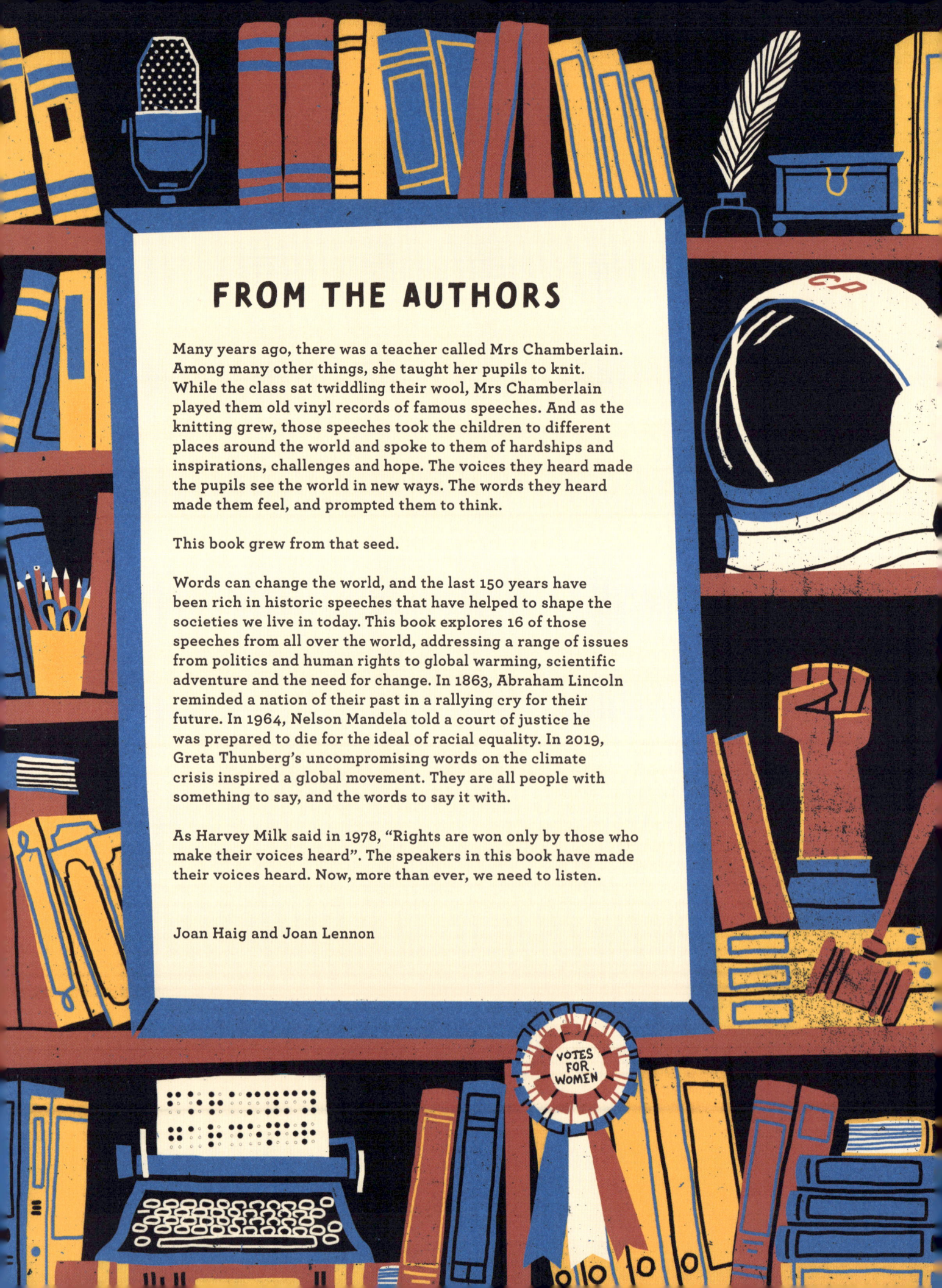

Many years ago, there was a teacher called Mrs Chamberlain. Among many other things, she taught her pupils to knit. While the class sat twiddling their wool, Mrs Chamberlain played them old vinyl records of famous speeches. And as the knitting grew, those speeches took the children to different places around the world and spoke to them of hardships and inspirations, challenges and hope. The voices they heard made the pupils see the world in new ways. The words they heard made them feel, and prompted them to think.

This book grew from that seed.

Words can change the world, and the last 150 years have been rich in historic speeches that have helped to shape the societies we live in today. This book explores 16 of those speeches from all over the world, addressing a range of issues from politics and human rights to global warming, scientific adventure and the need for change. In 1863, Abraham Lincoln reminded a nation of their past in a rallying cry for their future. In 1964, Nelson Mandela told a court of justice he was prepared to die for the ideal of racial equality. In 2019, Greta Thunberg's uncompromising words on the climate crisis inspired a global movement. They are all people with something to say, and the words to say it with.

As Harvey Milk said in 1978, "Rights are won only by those who make their voices heard". The speakers in this book have made their voices heard. Now, more than ever, we need to listen.

Joan Haig and Joan Lennon

ABOUT THE BOOK

This book is organised into chapters, each of which introduces you to a speech and tells you the story of who made it and why.

Many of the speeches were thousands of words long and some lasted hours, so they are not printed in full. Instead, we have chosen extracts that capture the main points. The parts of speech that are missing are shown by three dots (...).

Alongside each speech, you will find information that talks about the speaker's message and how they used words and language. This text is shown in *italics*.

If you get stuck on a difficult word or phrase, head to the glossary at the back of the book to find out what it means.

The book is set out in date order, but you can read it any way you like. At the end of each chapter, follow the signposts in the direction you want to go.

MEET THE SPEAKERS

10 — 'THE GETTYSBURG ADDRESS' 1863 — ABRAHAM LINCOLN

14 — 'FREEDOM OR DEATH' 1913 — EMMELINE PANKHURST

18 — 'AN ABORIGINAL WOMAN ASKS FOR JUSTICE' 1938 — PEARL GIBBS

22 — 'THEIR FINEST HOUR' 1940 — WINSTON CHURCHILL

26 — 'A TRYST WITH DESTINY' 1947 — JAWAHARLAL NEHRU

30 — 'A TALK ABOUT WOMEN' 1949 — FUNMILAYO RANSOME-KUTI

34 — 'THE LIFE AND LEGACY OF LOUIS BRAILLE' 1952 — HELEN KELLER

38 — 'FIRST FLIGHT OF A MAN INTO COSMIC SPACE' 1961 — YURI GAGARIN

42
'STATEMENT FROM THE DOCK' 1964

NELSON MANDELA

46
'THE CHARTER OF HUMAN RIGHTS' 1968

RENÉ CASSIN

50
'THE HOPE SPEECH' 1978

HARVEY MILK

54
'ADDRESS TO THE UNITED NATIONS YOUTH ASSEMBLY' 2013

MALALA YOUSAFZAI

58
'REMARKS BY THE PRESIDENT AT THE 50TH ANNIVERSARY OF THE SELMA TO MONTGOMERY MARCHES' 2015

BARACK OBAMA

62
'STATEMENT TO THE WHO WORLD HEALTH ASSEMBLY IN GENEVA' 2015

ANGELA MERKEL

66
'LISTEN TO THE CHILDREN' 1992 & 'OUR HOUSE IS ON FIRE' 2019

SEVERN CULLIS-SUZUKI & GRETA THUNBERG

72
GLOSSARY

... A NEW NATION, CONCEIVED IN LIBERTY, AND DEDICATED TO THE PROPOSITION THAT ALL MEN ARE CREATED EQUAL.

'THE GETTYSBURG ADDRESS'
ABRAHAM LINCOLN
1863

THE AMERICAN CIVIL WAR

The American Civil War (1861–1865) was fought between the northern states (the Union) and the southern states (the Confederacy) to decide the future of the nation. Abraham Lincoln was leader of the Union throughout the war.

19 November 1863

It was a cold, bright winter's day, just outside the little town of Gettysburg, Pennsylvania, USA.

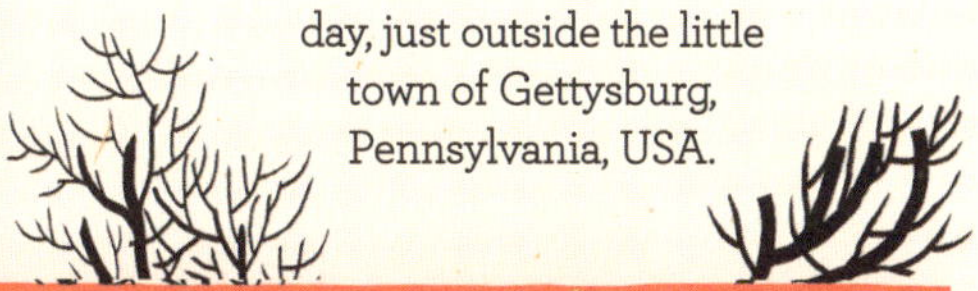

A few months before, thousands of soldiers had been killed nearby at the Battle of Gettysburg. Now, with the war still raging, huge crowds were gathering to honour them at the dedication of the Soldiers' National Cemetery.

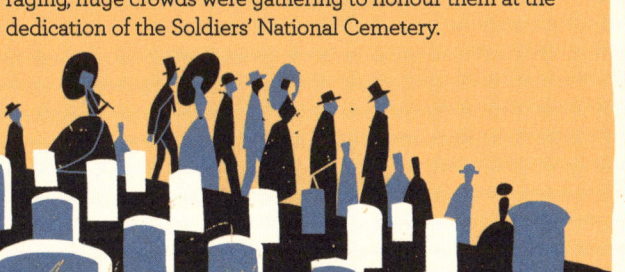

The Battle of Gettysburg began on 1 July 1863 and lasted for three long summer days. It was one of the bloodiest conflicts in the American Civil War.

But why were the Confederacy and the Union fighting? Wars always have more than one cause. The two sides had both been part of the United States of America, until disagreements over economics, politics, attitudes to slavery and different ways of life finally caused a divide. From 1860 to 1861, the 11 southern states of the Confederacy officially withdrew from being part of the country.

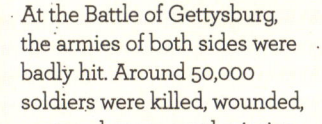

We want to be separate!

We need to stay together as a nation!

We need a powerful central government!

But we don't WANT a powerful central government!

We need slaves to make our plantations profitable!

But we want to abolish slavery!

At the Battle of Gettysburg, the armies of both sides were badly hit. Around 50,000 soldiers were killed, wounded, captured or reported missing.

During the four years of the American Civil War, more than 50,000 amputations were performed. Between operations, surgical instruments were wiped on the surgeon's sleeve.

As the fighting continued, medicine and anaesthetics kept running out. Whisky was often the only pain relief available.

For every soldier killed in battle during the American Civil War, two more died of disease.

The dedication of the Soldiers' National Cemetery at Gettysburg in 1863 was attended by six state governors and 15,000 spectators. Former US Secretary of State Edward Everett was the main speaker. He spoke eloquently about the horrors of the war, describing Confederate conspiracies and atrocities against the Union, and calling angrily for vengeance. After two long hours, he sat down to thunderous applause.

And then something extraordinary happened ...

'THE GETTYSBURG ADDRESS'
19 NOVEMBER 1863

President Abraham Lincoln began to speak. A little over two minutes later, he had already sat down again.

The speech was so short, the photographer didn't even have time to take a picture, and yet the words of Lincoln's 'Gettysburg Address' are remembered all over the world to this day.

Four score and seven years ago our fathers brought forth on this continent, a new nation, conceived in Liberty, and dedicated to the proposition that all men are created equal.

Now we are engaged in a great civil war ... We are met on a great battle-field of that war. We have come to dedicate a portion of that field, as a final resting place for those who here gave their lives that that nation might live ...

But, in a larger sense, we can not dedicate—we can not consecrate—we can not hallow—this ground. The brave men, living and dead, who struggled here, have consecrated it, far above our poor power to add or detract ... It is for us the living, rather, to be dedicated here to the unfinished work which they who fought here have thus far so nobly advanced. It is rather for us to be here dedicated to the great task remaining before us ... that this nation, under God, shall have a new birth of freedom—and that government of the people, by the people, for the people, shall not perish from the earth.

Lincoln's speech was perfectly paced for such a solemn occasion. Read it aloud and you will find you can't hurry. There were pauses built into the sentences to give the words time to sink in.

He used repetition in threes as a way of emphasising important ideas: "we can not dedicate—we can not consecrate—we can not hallow—this ground" and "government of the people, by the people, for the people".

Lincoln had complicated views on the issues behind the war, but in his speech, unlike Everett, he didn't talk about hating the enemy or abolishing slavery or getting revenge. Instead, with his opening sentence, he invited the audience to look back to 1776, to the Declaration of Independence. This was the document that marked the beginning of the United States of America, describing a new nation dedicated to equality, freedom and democracy. Then, with his closing sentence, Lincoln asked his listeners to look to the future, and to work towards a time when those ideals could be fully realised.

WHAT DID THE NEWSPAPERS SAY?

HARRISBURG PATRIOT & UNION
"We pass over the silly remarks of the President. For the credit of the nation we are willing that the veil of oblivion shall be dropped over them, and that they shall no more be repeated or thought of."

CHICAGO TIMES
"The cheeks of every American must tingle with shame as he reads the silly, flat, and dishwatery utterances."

SPRINGFIELD REPUBLICAN
"[President Lincoln's] little speech is a perfect gem; deep in feeling, compact in thought and expression, and tasteful and elegant in every word and comma … Turn back and read it over, it will repay study as a model speech. Strong feelings and a large brain are its parents."

CHICAGO TRIBUNE
"The dedicatory remarks by President Lincoln will live among the annals of man."

At the time, opinions on the Gettysburg Address and Abraham Lincoln varied. What the newspapers said about the speech depended on whether the editors – and their readers – had voted *for* or *against* Lincoln for President.

DID LINCOLN'S SPEECH AT GETTYSBURG END THE CIVIL WAR?

No. The war dragged on for two more years and, by its end in 1865, as many as 750,000 soldiers are thought to have died.

Lincoln was commander-in-chief of the Union for all four years of the vicious conflict. Like any war, nobody knew how it was going to end, or how the deep divisions of the nation could be healed, yet Lincoln held on to his innate kindness and gentleness.

During a major military campaign in early 1865, weeks before the end of the war, Lincoln was distracted at a meeting with a general by the unhappy mewing of kittens. He was heard to remark: "Kitties, thank God you are cats, and can't understand this terrible strife that is going on," and as he left, he asked an officer to make sure they were "given plenty of milk and treated kindly".

The American Civil War officially ended on 9 April 1865, but the divisions between the North and the South still remained. Five days later, while at the theatre with his wife, Abraham Lincoln was shot by Confederate supporter John Wilkes Booth. Lincoln died the next morning.

Lincoln's speech at Gettysburg was like a signpost, pointing his listeners back to where they had come from, and forwards to where they wanted to go. It is a reminder and a call to action still worth listening to.

Want to hear more about the legacy of slavery? Visit page 58

Want to hear more about inspiring war speeches? Visit page 22

Want to hear more about divided countries? Visit page 30

... WE WILL PUT THE ENEMY IN THE POSITION WHERE THEY WILL HAVE TO CHOOSE BETWEEN GIVING US FREEDOM OR GIVING US DEATH.

'FREEDOM OR DEATH'
EMMELINE PANKHURST
1913

In 1903, in the city of Manchester, UK, Emmeline Pankhurst and her eldest daughter Christabel founded the Women's Social and Political Union (WSPU). The organisation campaigned fearlessly for women's right to vote.

THE SUFFRAGETTE MOVEMENT

This wasn't the first time that women in Britain had fought for the vote. Since the mid-nineteenth century, female campaigners called 'suffragists' had tried to win rights for women in society through peaceful petitions and, later on, by refusing to pay their taxes.

But this campaign was slow with few results. After years of unsuccessful peaceful protest by the suffragists, the WSPU decided that it was time for action – 'Deeds Not Words', as their motto said. Members of the WSPU took part in 'civil disobedience' to literally fight for their cause. They chained themselves to railings, heckled politicians, placed bombs in empty buildings, and smashed windows in public places, constantly clashing with the authorities. They were so determined to achieve their political aims that they deliberately took part in violence and vandalism to influence the public and the government.

Newspapers began referring to militant WSPU campaigners as 'suffragettes'. By 1909, the WSPU had branches all over the country.

THE CAT AND MOUSE ACT

Around 1,000 suffragettes were imprisoned for their 'nuisance' behaviour. While in jail, some continued to fight by going on hunger strike, refusing to eat or drink. At first, they were released to prevent them from starving, but, by 1909, prison wardens began to force-feed them. Women were badly hurt, prompting public outrage at what was seen as government torture.

The government responded by passing the 1913 Prisoners' (Temporary Discharge for Ill Health) Act. Under this new law, when women on hunger strike became critically weak, they were sent home. As soon as they recovered, they were promptly rearrested to continue their sentence. It was dubbed the 'Cat and Mouse Act', likened to the way a cat plays with its prey, repeatedly letting it escape before catching it again.

Emmeline Pankhurst was imprisoned and released 11 times! It was in 1913, in between prison sentences, that she visited the United States to campaign for support and funding. She addressed a group of women at the Parsons Theatre in Hartford, Connecticut, in a powerful speech attempting to justify the use of militant tactics in the fight for women's rights.

'FREEDOM OR DEATH'

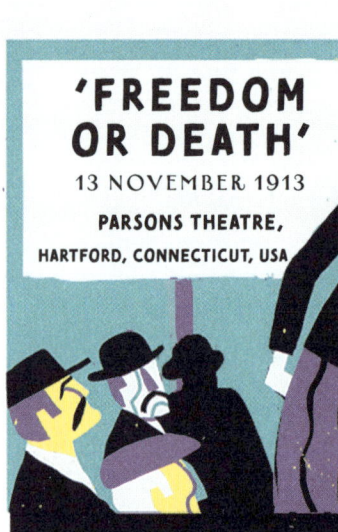

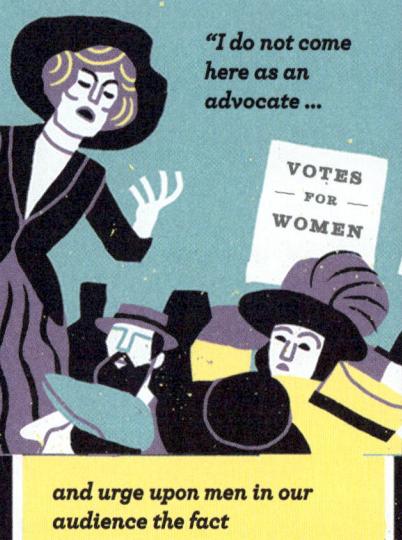

13 NOVEMBER 1913

PARSONS THEATRE, HARTFORD, CONNECTICUT, USA

"I do not come here as an advocate ...

I am here as a soldier ...

We women, in trying to make our case clear, always have to make as part of our argument,

and urge upon men in our audience the fact

— a very simple fact —

that women are human beings.

... We wear no mark; we belong to every class; we permeate every class ... and so you see in the woman's civil war the dear men of my country are discovering it is absolutely impossible to deal with it: you cannot locate it, and you cannot stop it.

... we will put the enemy in the position where they will have to choose between giving us freedom or giving us death.

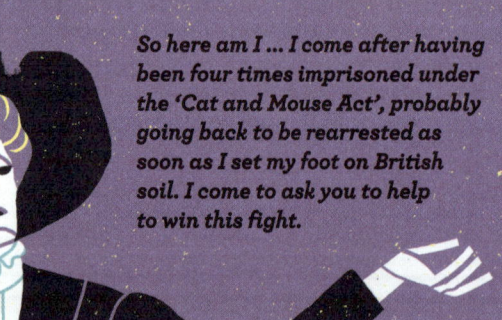

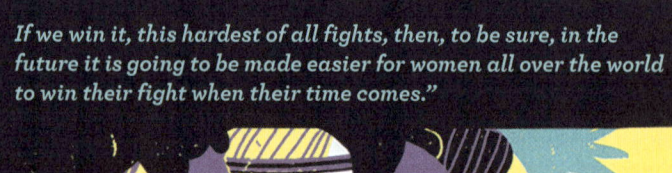

So here am I ... I come after having been four times imprisoned under the 'Cat and Mouse Act', probably going back to be rearrested as soon as I set my foot on British soil. I come to ask you to help to win this fight.

If we win it, this hardest of all fights, then, to be sure, in the future it is going to be made easier for women all over the world to win their fight when their time comes."

The "enemy" was the government in the cat-and-mouse chase. If the government did not grant women the right to vote, they would continue to die for the cause.

Pankhurst empowered individuals by putting them at the centre of a universal fight. She talked first about herself, then about the women at the rally ("we") and then about "women all over the world".

Pankhurst didn't go to the US to explain why women should fight for the vote; she went to convince them that the only way to win was to wage what she called "civil war". Her language was blunt, direct and forceful.

The feminist movement in the US was divided, like in Britain. Pankhurst aimed to rally together women from different political parties and social classes under one banner.

WOMEN IN WORLD WAR I

Much of Pankhurst's speech drew on the language of war, with words like "fight", "soldier" and "enemy". When World War I broke out in 1914, her words took on a different meaning: she encouraged women to join the war effort as a way to win the vote.

What is the use of fighting for a vote if we have not got a country to vote in?

But by the onset of WWI, Emmeline's other daughter, Sylvia, had become a pacifist – she believed that war and violence were unjustifiable.

War is callous and wicked!

We want peace and equal rights for ALL those who are disenfranchised!

By "disenfranchised", Sylvia meant everyone who didn't have the right to vote for their government – those who were seen as too poor or too ill, not just women. While her mother and sister found themselves linking women's suffrage to the fight for Britain, Sylvia found herself fighting for a wider social cause.

The War Effort

Women in Britain were not allowed to fight on the front line. Instead, two million women took up the jobs left by men who had been recruited as soldiers, and worked as ambulance drivers, bookkeepers and in factories.

The Women's Party

In 1917, Emmeline and Christabel transformed the WSPU into the Women's Party with the new motto: 'Victory, National Security and Progress'. They recruited men and women to fight against a common, foreign enemy – Germany. Sylvia, meanwhile, dedicated her time to helping women and the poor make ends meet.

1918 Representation of the People Act

People's collective effort during WWI forced the British government to change the law. The right to vote was extended to women aged 30 or older who owned property, women who were university graduates, and to all men over the age of 21. Women were also allowed, for the first time, to stand as Members of Parliament.

Universal Suffrage

In 1928, the same year that Emmeline Pankhurst died, aged 69, the government passed the Equal Franchise Act. Under this law, all women in the UK could finally vote in national elections, on exactly the same terms as men.

1914 · 1917 · 1918 · 1928

Want to hear more about how war can speed up change? Visit page 26

Want to hear more about women's rights around the world? Visit page 30

Want to hear more about death and freedom? Visit page 42

LADIES AND GENTLEMEN, I AM AN AUSTRALIAN.

ABORIGINAL PEOPLE CLAIM CITIZEN RIGHTS!

'AN ABORIGINAL WOMAN ASKS FOR JUSTICE'
PEARL GIBBS (GAMBANYI*)
1938

*Gambanyi is Pearl Gibbs' name in Ngiyambaa, the language of the Wangaibon and Weilwan peoples.

The first peoples of Australia are known to have lived and thrived across the continent for at least 65,000 years, developing many different cultures, customs and languages. In 1606, European invasion of Australia began on the west coast.

Nearly two centuries later, in 1770, a lieutenant in the British army, James Cook, invaded Australia's east coast to lay claim to the continent for Britain. Due to harsh laws that existed in England, which led to the overcrowding of prisons, Britain decided to send its convicts to Australia, to serve their sentences on the other side of the world. Free settlers followed soon after and Britain continued to invade the mainland, eventually taking over the whole continent and making it a colony. The colonisation of Australia devastated the many different groups of native Australians who became known collectively as Aboriginal, Indigenous or First Nations peoples.

HARD TIMES

Using modern guns, the settlers killed many thousands of Aboriginal people, sometimes slaughtering entire communities to steal land. Australia's original inhabitants also had no immunity to the new diseases the colonists brought with them and lost their lives in great numbers to tuberculosis, smallpox and other illnesses.

The Australian colonial government turned a blind eye to the massacres. They also ignored the right of Indigenous Australians to be counted in the country's census until 1967, cutting First Nations peoples off from federal services, including education and health care.

THE STOLEN GENERATIONS

By 1883, the settler authorities had set up 'Aboriginal Protection Boards'. These Boards were meant to provide food and medical aid to Aboriginal groups and to help them find work. But their real purpose was to control all aspects of their lives. The Boards forced Aboriginal groups off their land and on to reserves, handed out poor-quality food and destroyed traditional culture and lifestyles. Poverty and early death were common.

Between 1910 and 1969, government policies made it legal for Aboriginal children to be forcibly removed from their families. Most of these children were put into institutions to be trained as servants and labourers. The colonists tried to force First Nations children to reject their cultural heritage and languages, so they could fit into what the settlers saw as a superior society. The idea behind this was never equality, but to eliminate First Nations peoples and create a servant class for European colonists. These children became known as 'the Stolen Generations'.

PEARL GIBBS

Pearl Brown, later Gibbs, was born in 1901 in southeast Australia. A descendent of both Indigenous Australians and European colonists, she proudly described herself as "the grand-daughter of a full-blooded Aboriginal woman ... having lived and been with them as much as I have been with white people".

When Pearl left school, her job prospects were limited, so she worked as a domestic servant and a field labourer. She was appalled by the oppression that she saw around her. Pearl began to organise strikes among the Aboriginal women pea-pickers for better working conditions and arranged a boycott against a segregated local cinema.

Then, in Sydney in 1938, Gibbs was involved in the first major Aboriginal civil rights demonstration.

26 JANUARY 1788

On this day, Captain Arthur Phillip led the permanent invasion of Australia with the first shipload of British convicts and planted the flag of Great Britain, proclaiming it a colonial outpost of the British Empire. The local Eora people's name for this landing place was Warrane, but Cook had renamed it Port Jackson. The 26 January was celebrated by European settlers as First Landing Day, Foundation Day and then Australia Day. For First Nations peoples, it became known as Invasion Day or Survival Day.

26 JANUARY 1938

On this day, 150 years after the invasion began, Pearl Gibbs joined Aboriginal activists Jack Patten, William Ferguson and William Cooper in a mass protest, known as the Day of Mourning.

THE DAY OF MOURNING

The official Australia Day events included a sailing regatta, a lawn bowls tournament, a triumphant re-enactment of Captain Phillip's landing and a parade.

But Pearl Gibbs and many other Aboriginal rights campaigners had different plans to mark this day. Standing in the hot Australian sun, wearing formal black clothes, more than 1,000 supporters waited for the Australia Day parade to pass by, before marching silently from Sydney Town Hall to a conference in Australia Hall. Attendees had to enter by the back door of the hall, as the front door was for Europeans only. This meeting was for Aboriginal people only, to mourn the loss of their country, their freedom and the deaths of so many.

PEARL GIBBS SPEAKS

Pearl Gibbs was the only woman to address this first national Aborigines Conference at Australia Hall, and the last speaker of the day, but she made her voice heard. She spoke out passionately against the terrible conditions she had seen on Aboriginal reserves. Afterwards, memorial wreaths she had made were floated out to sea, as a symbol of 150 years of loss and oppression of Indigenous Australians.

AUSTRALIA DAY TODAY

Today, Australia Day is the official name for the holiday, although it is still known as Survival or Invasion Day. Every year on 26 January, in Sydney, many Australians flock to the Yabun Festival (Yabun means 'music to a beat' in Gadigal, a language of the Eora people), an alternative celebration with music, dancing, stalls and forums to commemorate the survival of Aboriginal culture. Here, everyone is welcome to celebrate all that it means to be Australian.

WOMAN TODAY

No.13   April 1938   Monthly 3.d

After the first Day of Mourning, Pearl Gibbs continued to campaign for Aboriginal rights, addressing non-Aboriginal audiences as well as Indigenous communities. Complete records of Gibbs' many speeches do not exist, but 'An Aboriginal Woman Asks for Justice' appeared as a letter in the magazine *Woman Today* in April 1938.

Gibbs understood the importance of the media to spread the message of equal rights, and made the first radio broadcast by an Aboriginal woman in 1941.

'AN ABORIGINAL WOMAN ASKS FOR JUSTICE'

1938

**Ladies and Gentlemen,
I am an Australian.
I have lived here all my Life.**

I love my country and I love its People. I wish something more for them than Riches and Prosperity. I wish for their greatness ...

We aboriginal women are intelligent enough to ask for the same citizenship rights and conditions of life as our white sisters ...

I am appealing to you on behalf of my people to raise your voices with ours and help us to a better deal in life ... in a word to grant [us] all the rights and responsibilities of DEMOCRACY.

When Pearl Gibbs introduced herself as an Australian, she was doing something subversive. With four simple words, she was challenging a mountain of colonial history and assumptions about what it meant to be Australian.

Gibbs was claiming her right to say "I am an Australian" based on the fact that she had lived in Australia all her life, but there was an emotional aspect as well. Her strong feeling for her country was part of what made her Australian.

In spite of everything that had happened to Aboriginal peoples, Gibbs was not preaching hate. She wanted her listeners to share her pride in Australia, and her hopes for its future.

It was common for non-Aboriginal Australian women to benefit from having low-paid Aboriginal servants. By addressing non-Aboriginal women as "my white sisters", Gibbs was challenging that relationship.

It was important that Gibbs included responsibilities along with rights. For too long, Aboriginal lives had been controlled by the Protection Boards. Indigenous Australians wanted to be allowed to act as accountable members of society.

BUILDING BRIDGES

Pearl Gibbs had a gift for bringing people together. As a campaigner, she acted as a link between Aboriginal and non-Aboriginal groups working for change. Gibbs carried on organising rallies, petitions and protests that eventually led to a landmark referendum in 1967 where the Australian people voted overwhelmingly for, among other things, Indigenous Australians to be included in the census. Gibbs was an active campaigner into the 1970s and she died in 1983.

Want to hear more about women and colonialism? Visit page 30

Want to hear more about the fight to be heard? Visit page 50

Want to hear more about love of your country? Visit page 38

21

'Their Finest Hour'
Winston Churchill
1940

Let us therefore brace ourselves to our duties and so bear ourselves that, if the British Empire and its Commonwealth last for a thousand years, men will still say, 'This was their finest hour'.

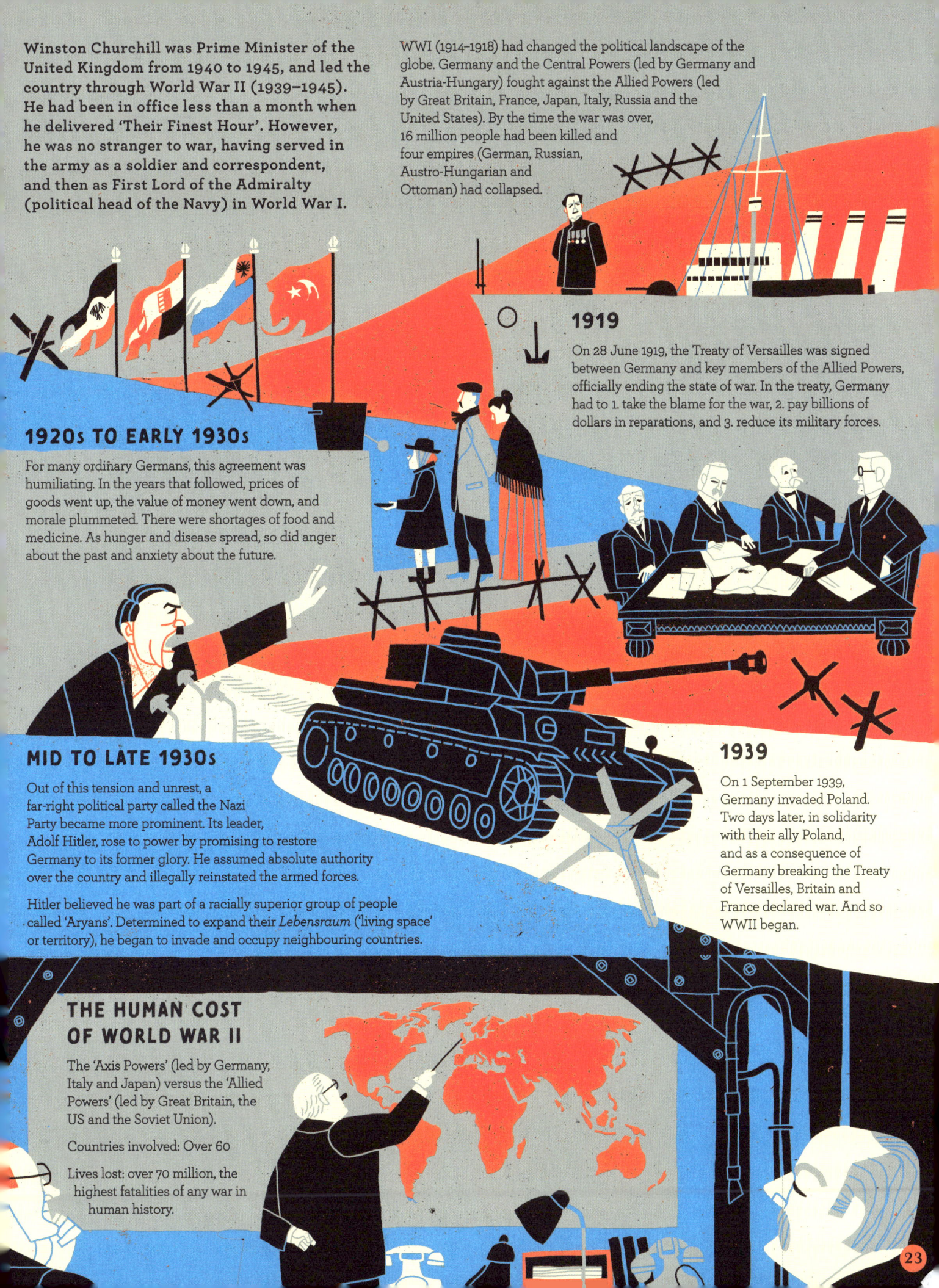

Winston Churchill was Prime Minister of the United Kingdom from 1940 to 1945, and led the country through World War II (1939–1945). He had been in office less than a month when he delivered 'Their Finest Hour'. However, he was no stranger to war, having served in the army as a soldier and correspondent, and then as First Lord of the Admiralty (political head of the Navy) in World War I.

WWI (1914–1918) had changed the political landscape of the globe. Germany and the Central Powers (led by Germany and Austria-Hungary) fought against the Allied Powers (led by Great Britain, France, Japan, Italy, Russia and the United States). By the time the war was over, 16 million people had been killed and four empires (German, Russian, Austro-Hungarian and Ottoman) had collapsed.

1919

On 28 June 1919, the Treaty of Versailles was signed between Germany and key members of the Allied Powers, officially ending the state of war. In the treaty, Germany had to 1. take the blame for the war, 2. pay billions of dollars in reparations, and 3. reduce its military forces.

1920s TO EARLY 1930s

For many ordinary Germans, this agreement was humiliating. In the years that followed, prices of goods went up, the value of money went down, and morale plummeted. There were shortages of food and medicine. As hunger and disease spread, so did anger about the past and anxiety about the future.

MID TO LATE 1930s

Out of this tension and unrest, a far-right political party called the Nazi Party became more prominent. Its leader, Adolf Hitler, rose to power by promising to restore Germany to its former glory. He assumed absolute authority over the country and illegally reinstated the armed forces.

Hitler believed he was part of a racially superior group of people called 'Aryans'. Determined to expand their *Lebensraum* ('living space' or territory), he began to invade and occupy neighbouring countries.

1939

On 1 September 1939, Germany invaded Poland. Two days later, in solidarity with their ally Poland, and as a consequence of Germany breaking the Treaty of Versailles, Britain and France declared war. And so WWII began.

THE HUMAN COST OF WORLD WAR II

The 'Axis Powers' (led by Germany, Italy and Japan) versus the 'Allied Powers' (led by Great Britain, the US and the Soviet Union).

Countries involved: Over 60

Lives lost: over 70 million, the highest fatalities of any war in human history.

GROWING FEAR

By the summer of 1940, Hitler had conquered Denmark, Norway, Belgium, the Netherlands, Luxembourg and France. The speed and ease of Hitler's conquests left the rest of Europe – and the rest of the world – in fear over what would happen next.

In June, Churchill addressed British politicians in the House of Commons. He needed to unite and reassure, but also to demand action. Germany and the Axis Powers were gaining strength and territory.

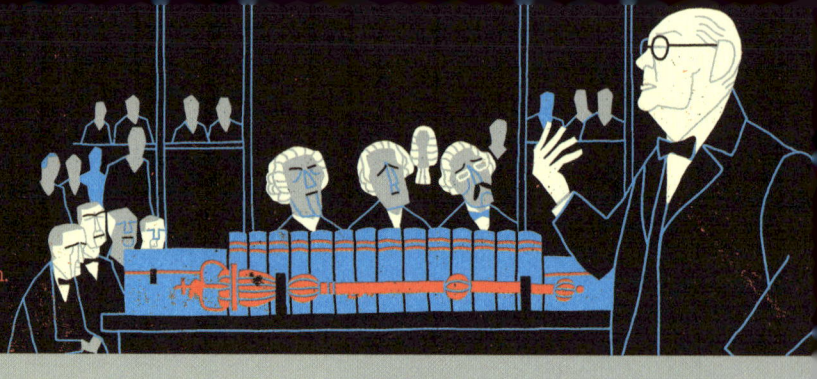

'THEIR FINEST HOUR'
18 JUNE 1940

Churchill wrote his own speeches, drafting and redrafting, practising and performing them.

He had them typed up in the way psalms appear in the Old Testament, making the pauses, pace and prose easier to learn by heart.

This punchy ending to Churchill's speech was a rallying cry to Britain and its territories around the globe.

> What General Weygand called the Battle of France is over. I expect that the Battle of Britain is about to begin...
> The whole fury and might of the enemy must very soon be turned on us.
> Hitler knows that he will have to break us in this Island or lose the war.
> If we can stand up to him, all Europe may be free, and the life of the world may move forward into broad, sunlit uplands.
> But if we fail, then the whole world... including all that we have known and cared for, will sink into the abyss of a new Dark Age made more sinister, and perhaps more protracted, by the lights of perverted science.
> Let us therefore brace ourselves to our duties, and so bear ourselves that, if the British Empire and its Commonwealth last for a thousand years, men will still say,
> "This was their finest hour".

Churchill used contrast to great effect. Present threat (the Battle of France) is weighed against future horror (the Battle of Britain). Victory and freedom are painted as "broad, sunlit uplands" while defeat is "the abyss of a new Dark Age".

The British Empire did not last one thousand years. After the war, countries that had fought for Britain now began to fight for their own national independence.

Churchill was a controversial figure. While many respect his leadership qualities, he could be brutal and was known to have racist views.

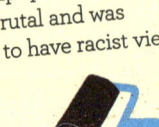

A DISTINCTIVE VOICE

Churchill became one of the most recognisable speakers in the world, partly because of his lisp and stammer. As a young man, he had worked with a therapist on 'correcting' his speech, repeating certain phrases, such as:

The Spanish ships I cannot see for they are not in sight ...

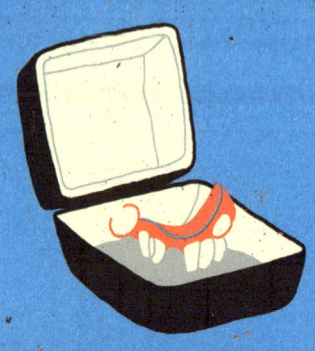

Later, as Prime Minister, he realised the value of having a distinct voice and way of speaking, especially on radio broadcasts. He even had special dentures (false teeth) designed to help him keep his lisp.

BATTLE OF BRITAIN, 1940

Churchill's speeches were broadcast on the radio, or 'the wireless' as it was known. In Britain, radio was the main form of communication between the government and the wider population, and the Home Service radio station provided updates on the war.

Churchill was a charismatic leader and his speeches boosted the nation's morale. Over 50 per cent of adults tuned in when he was on air. After Churchill's speech in June 1940, a Home Office report found British people felt more 'courageous and hopeful' than before, and a public poll in July showed that Churchill's approval rating had shot up to an impressive 88 per cent.

Just as well because, as Churchill had predicted, the 'Battle of Britain' began that summer.

SKY BOMBINGS

After successfully taking control of France, Hitler planned an invasion of England by sea, which was codenamed 'Operation Sealion'. To weaken British defences, Hitler decided first to attack by air with the Luftwaffe (the German air force). At the time, it was the biggest and strongest air force in the world. From July 1940, British airfields, harbours, factories and communication stations came under German fire.

THE BLITZ

On 24 August, Luftwaffe bombs were dropped over East London. Britain's forces retaliated by bombing the German city of Berlin. Furious, Hitler ordered mass air attacks on major cities across Britain, killing more than 40,000 civilians. The attacks, which began on 7 September, were known as the Blitz. Churchill used public appearances and broadcasts to promote the idea of a positive 'Blitz spirit' to encourage people not to give up hope.

FIGHTING FOR BRITAIN

Between July and October 1940, nearly 3,000 pilots, navigators and gunners from Britain, its allies and countries across the Commonwealth took to the air with the RAF (the UK's air force) in the Battle of Britain. It wasn't just airmen that braced themselves for their duties. Engineers, factory workers and ground crew repaired and prepared planes. Intelligence gatherers and codebreakers intercepted and decrypted Germany's top-secret messages, including the 'Enigma Code'. The Observer Corps and radar operators were on constant lookout for attacking aircraft.

In October, after three months of heavy fighting, Hitler called off the planned invasion of Britain. Although the Battle of Britain was over, the Blitz carried on into May 1941 and the war went on for a further five years. Churchill's speeches continued to bolster the spirits of soldiers and civilians alike.

Want to hear more about countries competing with technology? Visit page 38

Want to hear more about the need for international cooperation? Visit page 62

Want to hear more about the need for urgent action? Visit page 66

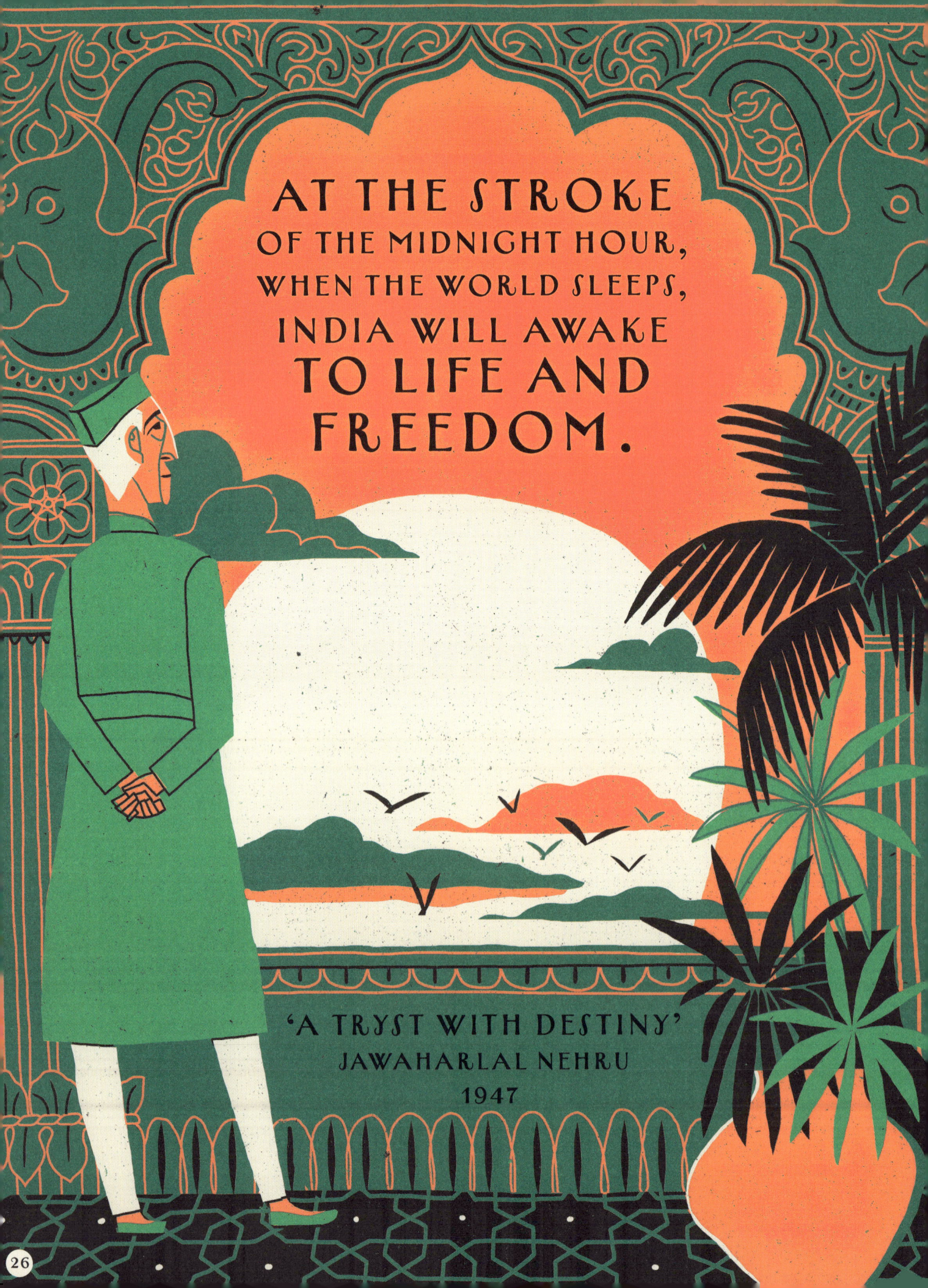

AT THE STROKE OF THE MIDNIGHT HOUR, WHEN THE WORLD SLEEPS, INDIA WILL AWAKE TO LIFE AND FREEDOM.

'A TRYST WITH DESTINY'
JAWAHARLAL NEHRU
1947

Throughout the nineteenth century, Britain's empire around the world was expanding. From 1858 to 1947, most of modern-day India, Pakistan, Bangladesh, Myanmar and Sri Lanka was ruled as part of the vast British Empire, which, by 1913, was the largest empire the world had ever known. Britain's reign over India was called the Raj.

During the Raj, conflict between the Indian people and their foreign oppressors was frequent and often bloody. The Indian people wanted change. In 1885, a political party called the Indian National Congress (Congress Party) began campaigning for freedom from British rule.

In 1947, the Congress Party won their political fight and the territory was divided into India and what is today Pakistan and Bangladesh. Jawaharlal Nehru, a young lawyer, became the first leader of the newly independent India.

THE RAJ

India was seen as the jewel in the British imperial crown. British companies had been setting up trading posts in India since the 1600s but the Raj meant Britain had even more control over the country's rich natural resources and prime locations on trade routes. In 1876, Queen Victoria gained the extra, newly invented title of Empress of India.

British-owned companies made a lot of money during the Raj by using cheap or indentured labour* to grow crops such as cotton, indigo, opium and tea for shipping to Britain and around the world.

For ordinary Indians, life was hard. British projects to build railways, roads and dams required huge numbers of labourers, who were badly treated. Famine became frequent as local farmers and land workers were forced to grow crops for export instead of planting extra food to keep them from hunger during droughts. On top of this, taxes were high. As the rich grew richer, ordinary Indians grew poorer.

* Indentured Labour
A system of labour where workers agreed, or were forced, to work for little or no pay for a set length of time, often for many years and often far away from home in foreign countries. They received payment or freedom, sometimes both, only at the end of that time.

DIVIDE AND RULE

To prevent the Indian people from joining together to rise up against them, British officials adopted a policy of 'divide and rule'. This meant they both reinforced and created class conflicts and religious tensions. For example, British officials helped wealthy Indian landowners suppress the voices of poor tenant farmers and brought in voting rules designed to keep Hindus and Muslims in separate political parties.

27

THE INDIAN INDEPENDENCE MOVEMENT

In 1885, as bitterness about British rule continued to grow, Indian leaders, who were mostly Hindus, came together to form the Congress Party. Its aim was to achieve 'Swaraj' or self-rule.

Indians of all religions supported Swaraj. Different people had different ideas about how it might be achieved. In some ways, lots of separate fights became one fight – the fight for independence.

I'm fighting for girls' and women's rights so we can join the struggle, too!

Woman

I'm going on strike! My landlord is forcing me to plant crops for British trade but paying me next to nothing. I refuse!

Tenant farmer

I'm sabotaging British settlers' property to scare them off and show them who is in command!

Rebel

I'm giving free legal advice to Indian people who have been wrongly arrested. The unfair court system has to end!

Lawyer

I'm teaching poor people English so they can speak for themselves – everyone needs to be heard!

Teacher

NEHRU AND GANDHI

In the later stages of the independence movement, Jawaharlal Nehru, a young Cambridge-educated lawyer from Allahabad in the northern Indian province of Uttar Pradesh, rose to prominence in Indian politics. He was appointed leader of the Congress Party in 1929.

Nehru's leadership was heavily influenced by his mentor, Mohandas Karamchand Gandhi (known as Mahatma, meaning 'great soul'), famous for his philosophy of peaceful protest.

We believe in non-violent non-cooperation.

This means Indians should refuse to buy British goods, obey British laws, pay taxes or attend British offices and schools.

It also means thousands of people will be arrested...

Nehru was imprisoned many times for civil disobedience, spending a total of nine years in jail.

INDEPENDENCE AND PARTITION

Nehru dreamed of a free India in which religion and politics would remain separate. Muslims and Hindus at first campaigned together for independence. However, the colonial setting intensified tensions between them. Many Muslims, members of India's largest minority, distrusted that they would be treated fairly in an independent state dominated by Hindus. From 1940, the Muslim League, a political party, led by Muhammed Ali Jinnah, campaigned for a separate, independent Muslim state, which would effectively divide India into two different countries.

World War II (1939-1945) changed Britain's relationships with its overseas territories. People from across the Empire were recruited to fight – and die – for Britain. While governments focused on the war, the Congress Party and Muslim League pushed for a transfer of power in India, and thousands died in violent clashes.

On 15 August 1947, the Raj officially ended. India and Pakistan (which included East Pakistan, now Bangladesh) were formed. Partition sparked widespread violence and one of the world's biggest refugee crises, as paramilitaries drove different religious groups across the new borders.

'A TRYST WITH DESTINY'

14 AUGUST 1947

Shortly before midnight on 14 August 1947, the eve of the countries' independence and his own appointment as India's first Prime Minister, Jawaharlal Nehru delivered an historic speech to the Indian Constituent Assembly in New Delhi, which celebrated India's freedom and looked to a new future.

Long years ago, we made a tryst with destiny; and now the time comes when we shall redeem our pledge, not wholly or in full measure, but very substantially. At the stroke of the midnight hour, when the world sleeps, India will awake to life and freedom.

A moment comes, which comes but rarely in history, when we step out from the old to the new — when an age ends, and when the soul of a nation, long suppressed, finds utterance …

Through good and ill fortunes alike, she [India] has never lost sight of that quest or forgotten the ideals which gave her strength. We end today a period of ill fortune and India discovers herself again …

And so we have to labour and to work, and work hard, to give reality to our dreams … We have to build the noble mansion of free India where all her children may dwell …

By "all her children", Nehru meant all Indian people. But he did believe children were vital to the nation. 'Chacha (Uncle) Nehru', as he was known by them, was passionate about improving their rights. His birthday (14 November) is celebrated in India as Bal Diwas – Children's Day.

Nehru began with the idea that India had made a tryst, an unspoken agreement, with the future that it would one day be free, acknowledging India's long history of foreign control. By saying "not wholly or in full measure" Nehru also acknowledged Partition, which he had worked hard to avoid.

Nehru believed the Indian nation had a "soul". He personified India and talked about it in feminine terms, drawing on Indians' love and loyalty towards their country, which had been known throughout the independence movement as 'Mother India'.

Nehru saw India's independence as an opportunity for it to become a democratic nation, where every person could vote for who was in power. His vision was for a modern, inclusive and industrialised society, which would require working together across divides.

NEW BEGINNINGS

The loss of the 'jewel' in Britain's imperial crown marked the end of over two centuries of British interference in India. It also marked the beginning of the end of the Empire. Nehru's speech celebrated independence as "a step, an opening of opportunity, to the greater triumphs and achievements that await us". As a world leader, he continued to campaign against colonialism, and for peace and dialogue.

Want to hear more about life under colonial rule? Visit page 18

Want to hear more about hope for a more inclusive future? Visit page 50

Want to hear more about speakers who were imprisoned? Visit pages 14 and 42

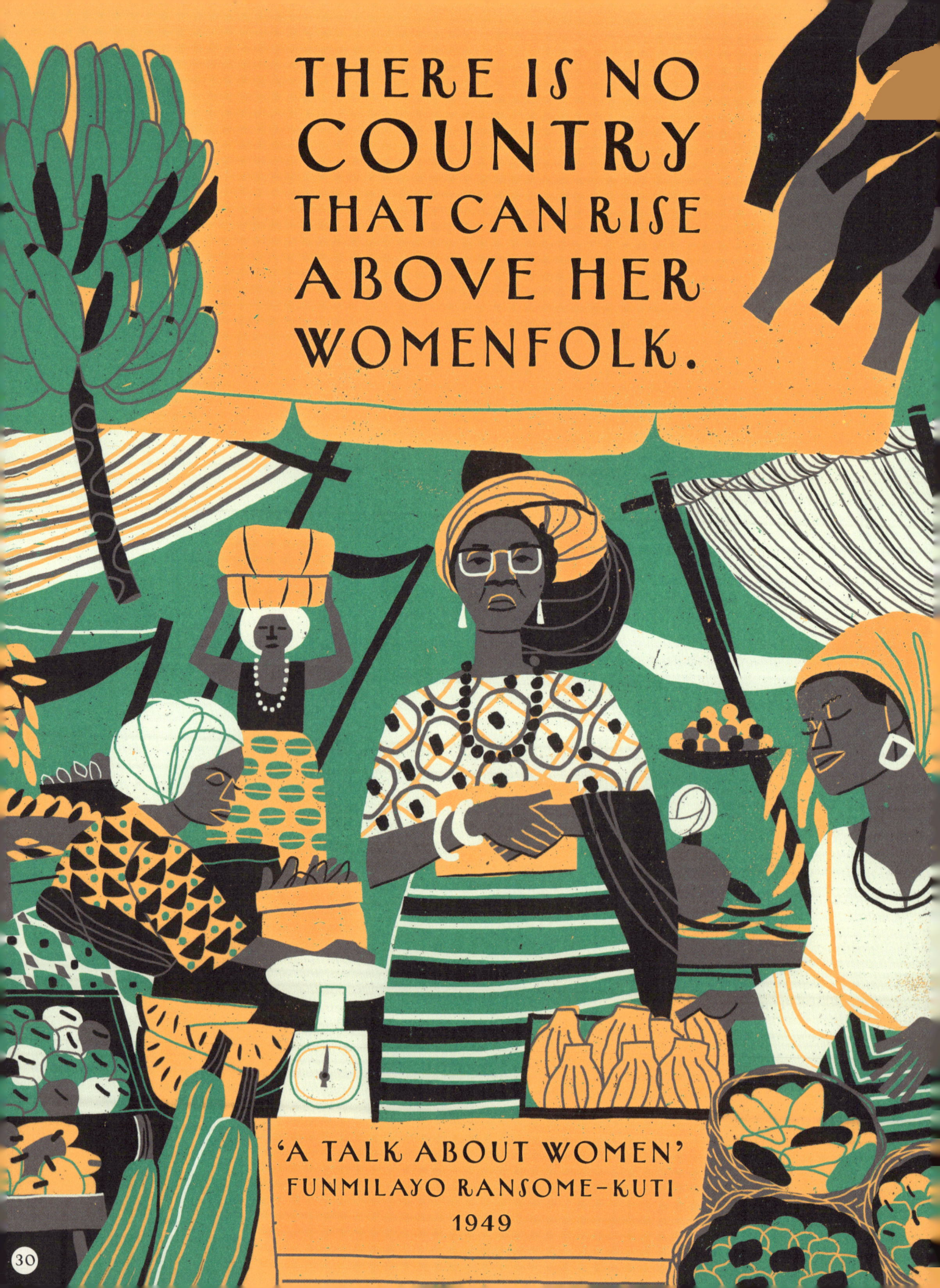

THERE IS NO COUNTRY THAT CAN RISE ABOVE HER WOMENFOLK.

'A TALK ABOUT WOMEN'
FUNMILAYO RANSOME-KUTI
1949

British interest in West Africa had begun with the slave trade in the 1600s and 1700s, but when that was abolished in 1807, they turned their attention to the area's other resources, such as cotton, palm oil, gold and oil.

THE SCRAMBLE FOR AFRICA

Towards the end of the 1800s, in what is known as the 'Scramble for Africa', the continent was carved up between Britain and other European powers, each eager to create an empire for themselves. This resulted in borders that were easy to draw on a map, but which took little account of the cultural and historical differences of the people who lived there. Britain seized control of large sections of Africa, including Nigeria.

AFRICA IN WORLD WAR II

The European powers forcibly set up colonies across Africa. During World War II (1939–1945), the demand for supplies and money to support the war effort grew.

In Nigeria, British officials targeted the market women – who traditionally controlled the local prices and flow of goods – by imposing gender-specific taxation (taxes that only applied to women) or simply taking their goods illegally. If the women couldn't pay the taxes or they objected, they were put in prison. The British also bolstered the power of the local male *alake*, or king, making it possible for him to treat the women in the same way.

ABEOKUTA WOMEN'S UNION

Born in 1900, Funmilayo Ransome-Kuti came from an educated, well-to-do Nigerian family. As a result, she was shielded from many of the injustices of colonial rule, but as an adult she saw what was happening to other Nigerians in her hometown of Abeokuta and refused to stand by.

She set up the Abeokuta Women's Union to bring together local women to fight for their rights. Understanding the importance of education, she held literacy classes for the market women, many of whom could not read or write. She also organised marches and protests against colonial rule, sometimes 10,000 women strong. When these demonstrations were banned, Ransome-Kuti called them 'picnics' instead and carried on. Imprisonment, as well as fines, tear gas and beatings, followed.

WHAT'S IN A NAME?

Born **Francis Abigail Olufunmilayo Thomas**, she was the granddaughter of a slave, but her father was a Nigerian Chief.

At the age of 19, she went to England to study. After returning, she dropped her English names **Francis Abigail**, re-asserting her African identity.

She married in 1925 and became **Funmilayo Ransome-Kuti**, which is the name she is best known by internationally.

In the 1940s, Ransome-Kuti's campaigning sparked the media to call her the **Lioness of Lisabi**, after the local warrior hero Lisabi.

In the 1950s, she became **Chief Funmilayo Ransome-Kuti**, a high-ranking title few women have achieved.

In 1970 she changed her surname from Ransome, a slave name, to **Anikulapo-Kuti**, as a symbolic rejection of colonial influence. Her work led her to become known to many as **'the Mother of Africa'**.

'A TALK ABOUT WOMEN'
1949

'A Talk about Women' is one of Funmilayo Ransome-Kuti's best-known addresses, though there is no record of exactly when or where it was given. In this speech, she wasn't aiming her words at the British colonial government. She was speaking directly to the Nigerian people.

HOW BEAUTIFUL WOULD IT BE IF OUR WOMEN COULD HAVE THE SAME OPPORTUNITY WITH MEN.

A PARENT WHO HAD MEANS TO EDUCATE A CHILD WOULD RATHER EDUCATE HIS OR HER SON, BECAUSE [THEY] BELIEVED HE WOULD BE RECEIVING [A] BIG SALARY WHEN HE HAD LEFT SCHOOL AND TOOK UP A JOB ... THE PARENT'S POOR DAUGHTERS ARE NEGLECTED AND LEFT UNEDUCATED BECAUSE THE PARENT FELT THAT WHATEVER EDUCATION SHE WAS GIVEN WOULD BE UNPROFITABLE AND WOULD ALL END IN THE KITCHEN ...

THESE POOR GIRLS EVENTUALLY BECOME RELEGATED TO THE BACKGROUND, ENSLAVED, ENFEEBLED, UNEDUCATED, IGNORANT AND ABSOLUTELY SILENCED AND SUPPRESSED IN OBSCURITY. THEY ARE OVERWORKED AND UNDERFED, YET THEY DON'T COMPLAIN, BECAUSE THEY ARE UNCONSCIOUS OF THEIR RIGHT ...

AS THERE IS NO COUNTRY THAT CAN RISE ABOVE HER WOMENFOLK, I AM THEREFORE APPEALING TO THE PARENTS ... TO GIVE THEIR DAUGHTERS EQUAL OPPORTUNITY WITH THEIR SONS.

Ransome-Kuti began her speech with a gentle way of speaking. She wasn't shouting at her audience, trying to start an argument or using aggressive language. The word "beautiful" feels positive and invites the listeners to see this idea in the same way.

She was saying that she understood how it had happened, that sons had seemed more profitable to their families than daughters, because women's roles in society were undervalued and under-paid.

She also wasn't blaming the women for not standing up for themselves. Without education, the women didn't know what their human rights were or how to demand them.

What does the phrase "there is no country that can rise above her womenfolk" mean?

Girls and women make up roughly half of any country. If half of the population are not allowed to contribute fully, the country will only be half as good as it could be. A country's greatness is dependent on every individual being able to reach their full potential, and for Funmilayo Ransome-Kuti, the key to that was education. In her speech, she appealed to Nigerian parents to educate their daughters as well as their sons, to help make Nigeria great.

TRAILBLAZER

Funmilayo Ransome-Kuti travelled internationally to campaign for women's rights and freedom from colonial rule. She helped create new schools in Nigeria and encouraged education for girls and women. She was the first woman in Nigeria to drive a car, opening the way for other women drivers. In 1947, she was the only woman included when a Nigerian delegation went to London, calling for independence and self-government.

NIGERIAN INDEPENDENCE

Independence from the British finally came in 1960. However, the newly independent Nigeria was faced with many challenges. Fierce divisions intensified between the north and south, two very different regions that had been grouped together under British rule as one country after the 'Scramble for Africa'. Religious conflict, economic problems, and violence and discrimination against women continued. Different military groups took over the government, before being overthrown themselves. As the new nation struggled to find its future, Funmilayo Ransome-Kuti continued to speak out for the rights of women and girls.

A FAMILY OF ACTIVISTS

The four children of Funmilayo and Israel Oludotun Ransome-Kuti became activists too, working to improve the lives of Nigerians through the fields of healthcare, education and music. Their son, Fela Kuti, was an internationally renowned musician and composer who pioneered Afrobeat and used his music to campaign against corruption and injustice. This brought him into conflict with the Nigerian government.

Funmilayo, then 78, was visiting Fela when his house was raided by Nigerian troops. She was thrown out of a second-storey window by the soldiers and later died of her injuries. Thousands attended her funeral, and the market women of Abeokuta closed their shops in her honour.

In 'A Talk about Women', Funmilayo Ransome-Kuti called upon the women of Nigeria to "strive to acquire knowledge in anything, from everywhere and anybody … to take the best from all that comes their way".

She never stopped believing in the power of education, and she remains an inspiration to Nigerians, Africans and the world.

THERE IS NO COUNTRY THAT CAN RISE ABOVE HER WOMENFOLK.

Want to hear more about fighting back against colonialism? Visit page 26

Want to hear more about other experiences of World War II? Visit page 22

Want to hear from another trailblazer? Visit page 34

'THE LIFE AND LEGACY OF LOUIS BRAILLE'

HELEN KELLER

1952

In the United States in the 1800s and early 1900s, blind children had limited opportunities. Most were sent to boarding schools to learn the poorly paid 'blind trades', including basket-weaving and brush-making.

He must make a living for himself...

...There is no other education for a child who can't see.

In 1880, Helen Keller was born into a wealthy family in Alabama, USA. She was a happy, healthy baby.

Then, at 19 months old, she fell ill and was left blind and deaf, with no way of learning how to speak. She was trapped behind a wall of darkness and silence.

Helen's family pitied and spoiled her, but no one knew how to help her. As the years passed, she grew into a violent child, so full of frustration and rage that she tyrannised the whole household.

One day in 1886, Helen's mother was reading Charles Dickens' *American Notes*, his travel diaries of North America.

In the book, Dickens mentions a blind-deaf child and a means of communication called 'finger spelling'. It sparked a hope in Helen's mother.

When Helen was six years old, Anne Sullivan came to live with the Keller family. Anne was sight-impaired and had grown up in a poorhouse until, at 14, she was accepted into the revolutionary Perkins School for the Blind in Boston, Massachusetts. When Anne graduated, the Kellers hired her and she took on the challenge of teaching Helen.

Anne started teaching Helen finger spelling, by making shapes with her hands to spell out words. At first, Helen couldn't understand the connection between the letter shapes and the objects she could feel. Wilful and angry, she fought Anne every step of the way, until ...

One day the breakthrough came when the two were pumping water outside the Kellers' house. Anne put one of Helen's hands into the cool liquid, while spelling out w-a-t-e-r into Helen's other palm, just as she had done for so many objects so many times before. Suddenly, as Anne described, "a new light came into her face". Helen made the connection between the shapes Anne was making in her hand and a word, and later wrote "my heart leaped". It was the first moment of a whole new way of understanding the world.

35

OPENING THE DOORS OF OPPORTUNITY

For Helen, the door to education and the world was now wide open. From finger spelling, she moved on to mastering Braille*, which meant she was able to read books, study, write and, later in her life, campaign for social change. In 1904, at the age of 24, she became the first blind-deaf person to graduate from university. (She studied at Radcliffe College for Women in Massachusetts, USA, because most universities at the time only accepted men.)

Helen Keller lived from 1880 to 1968. Her life bridged times of enormous change, from the aftermath of the American Civil War (1861–1865) through to the depths of the Cold War (1945–1991). Keller was able to use her education to respond to a shifting world and to champion causes such as votes for women, birth control, socialism, the fight against racism and an end to war. She travelled all over the globe to speak about these issues and never stopped fighting for the rights of others to get an education too, no matter what they had to cope with.

*WHO INVENTED BRAILLE?

During the Napoleonic Wars (1803–1815), a French officer called Charles Barbier came up with a system of raised dots called 'night writing'. This meant that soldiers could read combat messages by touch, without lighting a candle or a lamp that could give away their position and risk attack.

Louis Braille (1809–1852), a French teacher and inventor, lost his sight as a child, but longed to be able to read and learn. When he heard of Barbier's invention, Braille realised it could be made into a way for sight-impaired people to have access to specially produced books, using touch to decipher the words. Sixty years later, his system allowed Helen Keller to begin a rich, full life of reading, writing and learning.

HONOURED BY THE HOME OF BRAILLE

In 1952, Helen Keller was made a Knight of the Legion of Honour, one of the highest honours the French government can give, in recognition of her work in support of blind people all over the world. She was invited to accept her award and give a speech in Paris at the centennial commemoration of Louis Braille's death. Keller typed her speech on a Braille typewriter and delivered it in French.

'The Life and Legacy of Louis Braille'
21 June 1952

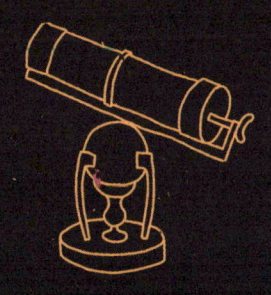

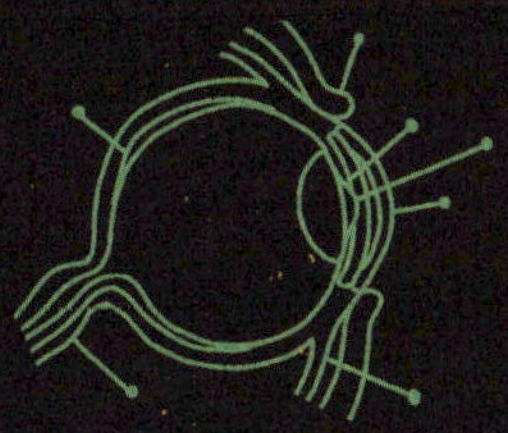

> In our way, we, the blind, are as indebted to Louis Braille as mankind is to Gutenberg. It is true that the dot system is very different from ordinary print, but these raised letters are, under our fingers, precious seeds from which has grown our intellectual harvest …
>
> The dismal doors of frustration would shut us out from the untold treasures of literature, philosophy and science. But, like a magic wand, the six dots of Louis Braille have resulted in schools where embossed books, like vessels, can transport us to ports of education, libraries and all the means of expression that assure our independence …
>
> Blind people of the world simply ask that where their abilities have been successfully put to the test, they are given the chance to participate fully in the activities of their sighted counterparts.

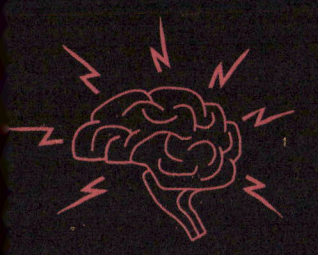

Invented in the 1400s, the Gutenberg Press allowed books to be printed in bulk for the first time, instead of each one being written by hand with quill and ink. It was the beginning of widespread access to reading, education and the spread of ideas, not just a few books for the very rich or the monasteries.

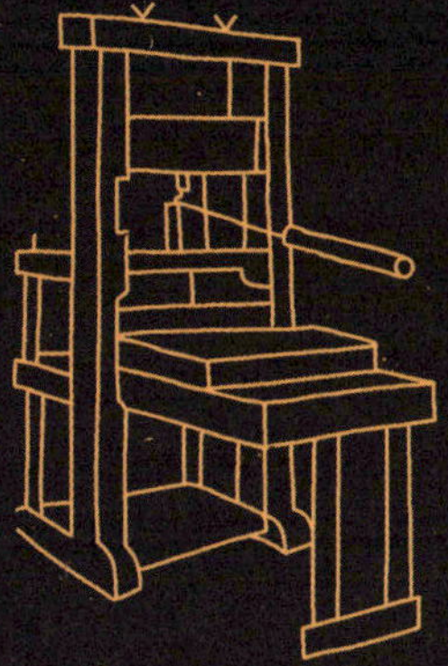

In her speech, Keller used words to paint a picture: "dismal doors", "precious seeds", "untold treasures". She made feelings vivid in her listeners' minds.

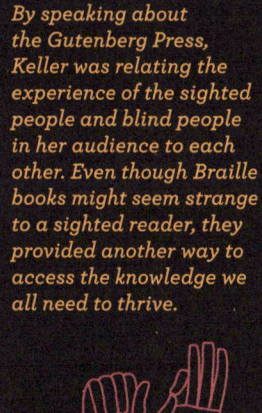

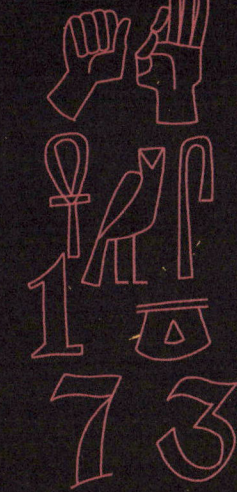

Keller was not asking for different standards to be applied to blind people, only that they be treated fairly.

By speaking about the Gutenberg Press, Keller was relating the experience of the sighted people and blind people in her audience to each other. Even though Braille books might seem strange to a sighted reader, they provided another way to access the knowledge we all need to thrive.

Though the battle for equal access to learning for all – girls and boys, disabled people and non-disabled people – continues, Helen Keller's message is to never lose hope: **"Although the world is full of suffering, it is full also of the overcoming of it."**

Want to know what the Braille message on page 34 says? Visit page 72

Want to hear more about education against the odds? Visit page 54

Want to hear more about speaking up for others? Visit page 46

THE EARTH IS SURROUNDED BY A CHARACTERISTIC BLUE HALO.

'FIRST FLIGHT OF A MAN INTO COSMIC SPACE'
YURI GAGARIN
1961

СССР (Союз Советских Социалистических Республик) = USSR (Union of Soviet Socialist Republics)

Yuri Gagarin was born in Russia in 1934 and grew up during World War II (1939–1945). Like many Russians, the Gagarin family suffered during the Nazi occupation. Their house was taken over by the German military, and they were forced to live in a tiny mud hut in the yard, while Yuri's older sister and brother were deported to labour camps in Poland.

THE COLD WAR

The USSR and the US had been allies during WWII, but then political differences and suspicions drove them apart. When WWII ended in 1945, the Cold War began. It was called a 'cold war' because the two superpowers didn't attack each other directly. Instead, they waged 'proxy wars', by supporting opposing sides of conflicts in places including Vietnam, Korea and Afghanistan.

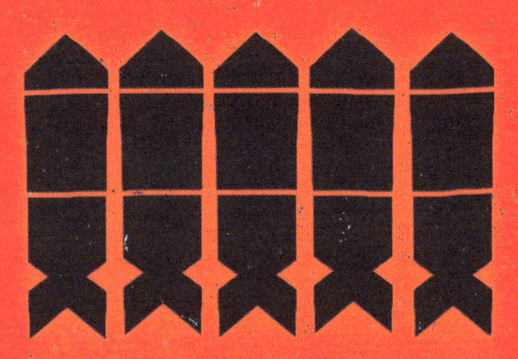

Meanwhile, huge amounts of money were spent by both sides to develop and stockpile more and more devastating nuclear weapons. During this time, there was real fear all over the world that human life would end in a nuclear holocaust. But perhaps what the Cold War is most remembered for is how two nations in competition launched humanity into outer space.

The Theory of MAD

During the Cold War, both the US and the USSR based their actions on the theory of MAD, Mutually Assured Destruction. This was the idea that if either side had the ability to wipe out the other, neither would fire the first shot.

After working in a steel factory, Gagarin enrolled in an Air Force flying school in 1955, aged 21. At just 1.57 metres tall, he had trouble seeing out of the cockpit window, and failed the landing tests twice. It was only when his instructor added a cushion for him to sit on that Gagarin landed successfully.

When he began training to be a cosmonaut in 1960, however, he was the perfect size for the cramped *Vostok* capsule in which he was to make the very first human flight into space.

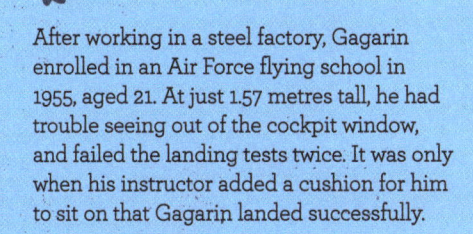

'FIRST FLIGHT OF A MAN INTO COSMIC SPACE'
15 APRIL 1961

On 12 April 1961, cosmonaut Yuri Gagarin launched from the Baikonur Cosmodrome in Kazakhstan (then part of the USSR) in *Vostok 1*, on the first human space flight. It took 108 minutes to orbit the Earth. Three days later, Gagarin gave a press conference in Moscow, where a NASA translator recorded his speech.

The clouds which cover the Earth's surface are very visible, and their shadow on the Earth can be seen distinctly ... The Earth is surrounded by a characteristic blue halo ... From a light-blue colouring, the sky blends into a beautiful deep blue, then dark blue, violet, and finally complete black ... The transition into the Earth's shadow took place very rapidly. Darkness comes instantly and nothing can be seen ...

I am immensely glad that my beloved fatherland was the first in history to penetrate [the] cosmos ... the first satellite, the first cosmic spaceship and the first manned flight into space, these are the stages on the great road of my fatherland toward the conquest of the mysteries of nature.

We plan to fly some more and intend to conquer cosmic space as it should be done. Personally, I would like to fly some more into space. I like flying. My biggest wish is to fly toward Venus, toward Mars, which is really flying.

We are now familiar with beautiful colour images of Earth from space, but Gagarin's flight was the first time a human had seen our world from this angle. There was no camera aboard Vostok 1. *Gagarin's audiences across the globe were fascinated by his description of what he saw. It united the world at a time when Cold War tensions threatened our future.*

At the same time, Gagarin was pressing home to his listeners the fact that the USSR had won this stage of the space race, repeating the word "first" again and again.

By describing the USSR as "my fatherland", Gagarin identified himself with the East, giving his patriotism an added layer of emotion.

1951
US Defense film *Duck and Cover* tells schoolchildren how to protect themselves from a nuclear bomb.

JANUARY 1958
US launches the Explorer 1 satellite.

MAY 1961
Alan Shepard is the first American in space, on board Freedom 7.

1945
World War II ends and the Cold War begins.

OCTOBER 1957
USSR launches Sputnik*, the first satellite in space.

APRIL 1961
Yuri Gagarin of the USSR becomes the first human in space, on board Vostok 1†.

AUGUST 1961
USSR builds the Berlin Wall, dividing the city between the East and the West. It becomes a symbol of the Cold War.

*Sputnik = travelling companion   †Vostok = east   *†Mir = peace, world, village

THE SPACE RACE

Throughout the Cold War, the USSR (the East) and the US (the West) tried to outdo each other in everything from technology, weapons, forms of government and ways of living. Part of this competition was the race to conquer space.

At first, the USSR pulled ahead, launching the first satellite and the first human into space. After that, landing a person on the Moon became the focus of the race, and the US invested more and more resources into achieving that goal. When US astronaut Neil Armstrong stepped out onto the surface of the Moon in 1969, it was a moment that captured the imagination of the whole world.

Many things we're familiar with today use technology originally developed for the space race, including portable computers, medical CAT scanners, LED lights, communication satellites and even freeze-dried food.

YURI GAGARIN'S LEGACY

After his historic achievement in 1961, Gagarin became a world celebrity and an ambassador for the Soviet space programme. His warm smile and friendly nature added to his popularity with the public.

However, after the USSR's *Soyuz 1* spacecraft went down in 1967, killing cosmonaut Vladimir Komarov, Gagarin was never allowed back into space. He trained again as an aeroplane pilot. Then, just five weeks after passing his retraining, his plane crashed and he died.

Every year, Gagarin's legacy is celebrated all over the world on 12 April. Yuri's Night is an opportunity for all of us to look up into the sky and be filled with the same wonder he felt.

Want to hear more about Earth's 'blue halo'? Visit page 66

Want to hear more about the Cold War? Visit page 46

Want to hear more about innovations that came out of war? Visit page 34

OCTOBER 1962
Cuban Missile Crisis
USSR installs nuclear weapons in Cuba, within range of mainland US. War is narrowly avoided when the weapons are removed 13 days later.

JULY 1969
US lands the first human on the Moon. (After losing the race to the Moon, USSR focuses on creating a crewed space station.)

FEBRUARY 1986
USSR launches the space station Mir*†. It is visited by scientists from many nations who conduct 23,000 experiments.

1991
A crumbling economy and dissatisfied countries within the USSR lead to its break-up and the end of the Cold War.

JUNE 1963
Valentina Tereshkova of the USSR becomes the first woman in space.

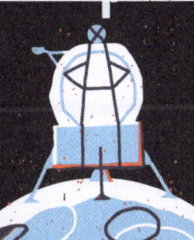

JUNE 1983
Sally Ride becomes the first American woman in space.

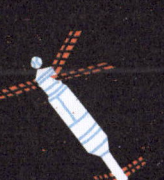

NOVEMBER 1989
The Berlin Wall comes down, symbolising hope for the future.

41

IT IS AN IDEAL WHICH I HOPE TO LIVE FOR AND TO ACHIEVE. BUT IF NEEDS BE, IT IS AN IDEAL FOR WHICH I AM PREPARED TO DIE.

STOP APARTHEID NOW

MANDELA for FREEDOM

APARTHEID IS OPPRESSION

'STATEMENT FROM THE DOCK'
NELSON MANDELA
1964

Born in July 1918 in Mvezo, South Africa, Rolihlahla (later, Nelson) Mandela dedicated his life to fighting racial discrimination. For centuries, white colonialists in South Africa had governed the country, organising the population into 'racial' groups and discriminating against people classed as 'non-white'.

In 1944, at the age of 26, Mandela was a newly trained lawyer and took an active role in the youth wing of the African National Congress (ANC), an organisation that strived for racial equality and promoted peaceful protest.

INEQUALITY IN SOUTH AFRICA

In 1948, the white-run National Party came to power in South Africa and took the racial divide one step further by introducing a policy of 'apartheid' (meaning 'apartness' in Afrikaans).

'Non-white' people (the majority of the population) were denied basic human rights and faced restrictions in every aspect of their lives, from where they could live to who they could marry.

THE SHARPEVILLE MASSACRE

In March 1960, in the black township of Sharpeville, white police opened fire on unarmed protesters, killing 69 people. The crowd had been demonstrating against pass laws, which were laws that restricted free movement of 'non-white' people within the country. The following month, the government made it illegal to form or be part of any group opposing apartheid.

AFTER SHARPEVILLE

In response to the massacre, some ANC members, including Mandela, decided that peaceful protest was no longer enough. They formed a secret organisation known as *Umkhonto we Sizwe* (meaning 'Spear of the Nation'), or MK. It was important for members to operate separately from the ANC, whose core goal was to bring about change without violence. In contrast, MK trained and prepared for armed struggle. They also attacked the infrastructure of the apartheid regime, for example, by destroying electricity pylons and government offices. Mandela claimed that MK only used violence as a last resort.

LILIESLEAF FARM RAID

In 1961, top leaders of MK bought a remote farm called Liliesleaf in the Rivonia area, north of the city of Johannesburg, to use as a covert meeting place and hideout.

In 1963, following a tip-off, the government's special forces raided Liliesleaf, making arrests and seizing weapons and top-secret documents. There was enough evidence to charge 11 members of MK, including Mandela, with treason and acts of sabotage.

Nelson Mandela, Walter Sisulu, Ahmed Kathrada, Govan Mbeki, Denis Goldberg, Raymond Mhlaba, Lionel Bernstein, Bob Hepple, Elias Motsoaledi, James Kantor, Andrew Mlangeni

CHARGED

The 11 men were eventually charged with taking part in 221 acts of sabotage intended to bring about violent revolution against the South African state. If found guilty, they could face the death penalty. The trial of the 11 MK members became known as the Rivonia Trial and lasted from 9 October 1963 to 12 June 1964.

'STATEMENT FROM THE DOCK'
20 APRIL 1964

On 9 October 1963, Nelson Mandela appeared before the Supreme Court in Pretoria, South Africa. As he walked into the courtroom, he raised a clenched fist – a sign of black solidarity.

On 20 April 1964, Mandela, as the first accused, gave a statement from the dock addressing the court. Doing so meant that he could not give evidence in his defence, but neither could he be cross-examined by the prosecution. Mandela spoke to the court for four hours, arguing that the court he was standing in needed itself to be judged, because it did not treat all South Africans equally. He delivered this address despite knowing that he might be sentenced to death.

Africans want to be paid a living wage … Africans want to be allowed out after eleven o'clock at night and not to be confined to their rooms like little children. Africans want to be allowed to travel in their own country … Africans want a just share in the whole of South Africa; they want security and a stake in society …

The ANC has spent half a century fighting against racialism … Their struggle is a truly national one. It is a struggle of the African people, inspired by their own suffering and their own experience. It is a struggle for the right to live.

During my lifetime I have dedicated myself to this struggle of the African people … I have cherished the ideal of a democratic and free society in which all persons live together in harmony and with equal opportunities. It is an ideal which I hope to live for and to see realised. But if needs be, it is an ideal for which I am prepared to die.

Through repeating the same phrase – "Africans want" – at the start of every sentence, Mandela emphasised the basic rights that Africans did not have.

It was how the accused had been fighting – sabotage, terrorism, training for guerrilla warfare – that was under scrutiny in court. But Mandela left this out, emphasising instead the ideals behind the cause.

For his final paragraph, Mandela put down his papers and appealed directly to the judge. He emphasised freedom, harmony and equality. There is a strong sense of balance: the individual and the people; hope for life and acceptance of death if convicted.

Mandela's closing words prompted gasps from the public gallery, followed by a long spell of silence and then the sound of crying.

THE VERDICT

The trial continued for two more months, closing on 12 June 1964. Mandela was 46 years old. He and seven others were found guilty, but the judge offered leniency by sparing them the death penalty and sentencing them instead to life imprisonment. (The death penalty would have caused massive and widespread outrage among the 'non-white' majority in South Africa, and the judge knew that the whole world was watching. MK, Nelson Mandela and the Rivonia Trial had gained huge media coverage around the world.)

Outside the courthouse, thousands of supporters had gathered, some shouting, "Amandla!" ("Power!") and others responding, "Ngawethu!" ("To the people!").

LONG WALK TO FREEDOM

Denis Goldberg, the only white political prisoner amongst those convicted, was incarcerated in Pretoria Central Prison on the mainland. Mandela and the others were flown to Robben Island, a maximum security jail 11 kilometres offshore from the Western Cape region of South Africa.

Mandela's cell had concrete walls, a small barred window and a light bulb that was lit day and night. In his memoirs, he wrote, "I could walk the length of my cell in three paces".

While incarcerated, Mandela became a symbolic leader of the ANC. The ANC continued its non-violent struggle against apartheid, putting pressure on the international community to boycott South African goods. In 1982, after 18 years on Robben Island, Mandela was moved to Pollsmoor Prison in Cape Town, where his family was finally allowed to visit him.

On 11 February 1990, aged 71 and after 27 years behind bars, Mandela walked free.

In 1989, F.W. de Klerk won the presidency of South Africa. His policies were a shift away from apartheid. He lifted the ban on opposition groups and ordered the release of ANC prisoners.

Following intense negotiations led by de Klerk and Mandela, a peaceful transition to democracy in South Africa was agreed, bringing decades of apartheid and white minority rule to an end. For this, they were jointly awarded the Nobel Peace Prize in 1993.

One year later, in South Africa's first democratic election, Mandela was voted in as the country's first black president.

Want to hear more about dedication to democracy? Visit page 18

Want to hear more about fighting racism? Visit page 58

Want to hear more about the importance of hope? Visit page 50

THE TIME HAS COME TO PROCLAIM THAT, FOR THE ESTABLISHMENT OF PEACE AND HUMAN DIGNITY, EACH OF US MUST WORK AND FIGHT TO THE LAST.

'THE CHARTER OF HUMAN RIGHTS'
RENÉ CASSIN
1968

René Cassin was born in Bayonne, France, in 1887. He was a brilliant young student and became a successful lawyer.

When World War I broke out in 1914, Cassin joined the army. He was badly wounded in 1916, but his life was saved by his mother, a field hospital nurse, when she insisted surgeons operate on him. After the war, Cassin began to realise that the consequences were as bad as the conflict itself. He saw disabled soldiers and orphaned children without proper support or help to rebuild their lives, and he decided to join the campaigns for better rights.

From 1924 to 1938, Cassin worked with the League of Nations – an international organisation which, among other goals, tried to solve disputes between nations to prevent wars.

In 1940, after France came under German control during World War II (1939–1945), Cassin made the difficult decision to leave his home country and go to London to help set up and run the French government-in-exile. He was an important part of many committees, where his legal expertise was invaluable.

Meanwhile, in France, his sister and other members of his family were killed by the Nazis because they were Jews. Yet, in spite of this terrible loss, Cassin believed that human rights, such as the right to a fair trial, were universal, even for those who committed atrocities.

THE UNIVERSAL DECLARATION OF HUMAN RIGHTS

This would become an historic document, but creating a statement of human rights that could apply to all people and all countries in the world was no easy undertaking.

The Commission had members from 18 different countries, each with their own cultures, traditions and beliefs. Not every country had the same views on all things, such as the rights of women, but for the declaration to work, everyone needed to agree on a set of basic universal standards.

Another part of the challenge was making it absolutely clear what each section, or 'article', meant. Vague advice like 'be nice to each other' would be so open to interpretation that it could end up meaning very little.

With his years of legal experience, Cassin played an essential role in finding the right words and the best ways for the members to reach agreement, at a time when the Cold War was beginning to divide the world more and more. But finally, in 1948, after two years of work, the UDHR was approved by the United Nations General Assembly after 48 of the 58 member nations at that time voted in favour. It went on to influence many treaties and laws aimed at improving human rights all over the world.

THE UNITED NATIONS

In 1945, in response to the horrors of WWII, 51 nations signed a declaration that vowed to create an international peacekeeping organisation. The United Nations (UN) was formed.

Carrying on from his work with the League of Nations, Cassin was involved in the United Nations from the beginning, as a representative of France and a well-respected lawyer.

Then, in 1946, Cassin was asked to join the UN's Commission on Human Rights. One of the Commission's tasks was to create a Universal Declaration of Human Rights (UDHR).

Declaration
The UDHR is a charter, not a law. A charter is a formal statement that can then be put into practice by governments of individual countries.

CASSIN'S NOBEL PEACE PRIZE

The year 1968 was declared the International Year of Human Rights. The aim was to bring attention to the state of human rights throughout the world, focusing on what had been achieved since 1948 and how far humanity still had to go.

On 11 December 1968, exactly 20 years after the completion of the UDHR, René Cassin was awarded the Nobel Peace Prize in recognition of his work on the charter that had laid the groundwork for so many of those achievements. He gave his acceptance speech in the Domus Media building at the University of Oslo, Norway.

'THE CHARTER OF HUMAN RIGHTS'

11 December 1968

There are fundamental liberties and rights common to all human beings, without possible discrimination.

… the organizing of peace must be based on considerations of reason … It presupposes tremendous efforts to modify through education some longstanding mental attitudes …

But reason alone is not enough. Emotional factors and especially the sense of justice must not be left to those who pervert them to the service of hate and destruction …

During the years of anguish when the freedom of whole peoples was in jeopardy, they were asked to persevere to the last. The time has come to proclaim that, for the establishment of peace and human dignity, each of us must work and fight to the last.

Cassin summarised the UDHR simply and powerfully to his audience, stating that all humans, without exceptions, have the same rights and freedoms. But there was nothing simple about the task Cassin and the rest of the Commission on Human Rights had set themselves.

He highlighted the importance of "education", "reason" and "sense of justice" in "the organizing of peace". By learning how to consider information carefully, we can begin to think about and challenge the existing ideas that our cultures have passed down to us.

Cassin and many of the people in his audience had lived through two World Wars, and at the time the Cold War was ongoing. They had seen how many atrocities during these conflicts had been justified and encouraged by noble-sounding lies. By speaking about their experiences, Cassin tapped into these powerful emotions to reclaim them for those who were working for peace.

Cassin spoke for a long time, and much of his speech had been formal and academic, describing a series of political processes and issues. But in his final paragraph, the passion that had kept him working so hard for so long shone through, as he called the world to action.

THE UNIVERSAL DECLARATION OF HUMAN RIGHTS

Article 1 Everyone is born free and equal.

Article 2 Everyone, without discrimination, has these rights.

Article 3 Everyone has the right to life, freedom and safety.

Article 4 Everyone has the right to freedom from slavery.

Article 5 Everyone has the right to freedom from torture.

Article 6 A person has these rights no matter where they are in the world.

Article 7 Everyone is equal before the law.

Article 8 The law protects everyone.

Article 9 No person shall be unfairly imprisoned or exiled.

Article 10 Everyone has the right to a fair trial.

Article 11 Everyone shall be considered innocent until proven guilty.

Article 12 Everyone has the right to privacy.

Article 13 Everyone has the right to free movement and travel.

Article 14 Everyone has the right to seek safety in another country.

Article 15 Everyone has the right to a nationality and to change it.

Article 16 Every adult has the right to marry and have a family.

Article 17 Everyone has the right to have belongings and to keep them.

Article 18 Everyone has the right to their own beliefs and to religion.

Article 19 Everyone has the right to think and express their thoughts freely.

Article 20 Everyone has the right to meet with others peacefully.

Article 21 Every adult has the right to take part in government and to vote.

Article 22 Everyone has the right to have their basic living needs met.

Article 23 Every adult has the right to a job, a fair wage, and to join a trade union.

Article 24 Everyone has the right to rest and relax.

Article 25 Everyone has the right to decent living standards.

Article 26 Everyone has the right to be educated.

Article 27 Everyone has the right to participate in culture and to have their own creations protected.

Article 28 Everyone's rights shall be recognised and respected.

Article 29 Everyone has responsibility to respect and protect the rights of others.

Article 30 No person or government can take away these rights.

> "There will never be peace on this planet as long as human rights are being violated in any part of the world."

To mark the International Human Rights Year in 1968, Cassin wrote a magazine article about the UDHR. He ended it with these warning words: "Now that we possess an instrument capable of lifting or easing the burden of oppression and injustice in the world, we must learn to use it."

The UDHR has been translated into over 500 languages and continues to be an invaluable tool in the fight for human rights.

We are still learning how to use it.

Want to hear more about the Cold War? Visit page 38

Want to hear more about some other Nobel Peace Prize winners? Visit pages 42 and 54

Want to hear more about thinking globally? Visit page 62

... IF A GAY PERSON MAKES IT, THE DOORS ARE OPEN TO EVERYONE.

'THE HOPE SPEECH'
HARVEY MILK
1978

The LGBTQ community – people who identify as lesbian, gay, bisexual, transgender or queer – has faced discrimination for centuries. From 1952 to 1973, homosexuality was listed as a mental disorder in the United States by the American Psychiatric Association. And it was illegal to be gay in many states until 2003.

For years, 'coming out' could mean losing your job, being disowned by family and friends, or being the victim of violent hate crimes.

In 1969, the Stonewall Riots were sparked when police raided a gay bar in New York City. Raids on gay bars were commonplace in the 1960s, but that night the customers of The Stonewall Inn fought back. The violent protests that followed marked the beginning of a more assertive reaction to police oppression of gay people.

In 1977, the celebrity and popular singer Anita Bryant spoke out publicly against gay people, calling them "evil forces around us". Many backed Bryant's anti-gay activism, but her words also stirred up support for the gay community and their fight for their rights.

In 1978, conservative politician John Briggs put forward Proposition 6, an initiative to ban gay people or anyone who supported their rights from teaching in schools in California. It attracted a lot of attention nationally and internationally.

Who was Harvey Milk?

Harvey Milk was born in New York City in 1930, into a prosperous Jewish family. He joined the Navy in 1951 as a diving officer aboard a submarine rescue ship.

In 1955, Milk was dismissed from the Navy with an 'other than honourable discharge'. This was probably because they suspected he was gay, which was banned in the military. He went on to work as a high school teacher, in the theatre, in insurance and on Wall Street, the financial centre of the US.

In 1973, age 43, Milk moved to San Francisco and opened a camera store. He was becoming more and more drawn to politics. As he said, "I finally reached the point where I knew I had to become involved or shut up". This was the beginning of Milk's journey as a key campaigner and spokesperson for gay rights.

Pride Parades

Marking the one-year anniversary of the Stonewall Riots, 1970 was the first year of gay pride parades in the US, calling for political change and publicly celebrating diversity. Today, hundreds of cities around the world have annual pride parades.

Rainbow Flags

In 1978, Milk challenged artist Gilbert Baker to create a symbol for gay pride. Baker's original eight-colour rainbow flag was unfurled at the San Francisco Gay Freedom Day Parade in the same year. Today, the six-colour flag is more common.

51

SUPERVISOR MILK

In 1973, Harvey Milk decided to run for public office. In November 1977 – on his fourth try – he succeeded. He was elected as one of 11 supervisors for San Francisco City Hall, even though campaigns against him had been loud and angry, and had included death threats. The following June, as part of the San Francisco Gay Freedom Day Parade, Milk stood on the steps of the same City Hall and spoke to a huge crowd. He asked:

Why are we here? Why are gay people here? And what's happening?

'THE HOPE SPEECH'
25 JUNE 1978

In 1977, gay people had their rights taken away from them in Miami. But you must remember, that in the week before Miami and the week after that, the word 'homosexual' or 'gay' appeared in every single newspaper in this nation ... everybody was talking about it, good or bad. Unless you have dialogue, unless you open the walls of dialogue, you can never reach to change people's opinion ...

Without hope, not only gays, but the blacks, the seniors, the handicapped ... will give up. And if you help elect ... more gay people, that gives a green light to all who feel disenfranchised, a green light to move forward. It means hope to a nation that has given up, because if a gay person makes it, the doors are open to everyone.

In footage of Milk's public appearances, he can be seen smiling and making eye contact, expressing energy and enthusiasm. He spoke as though he was having a personal conversation with each of his listeners. Milk believed that dialogue was the way forward. If we aren't talking to one another, there is no chance of changing anyone's mind.

Milk saw himself as representing all the voiceless people in his society – black people, older people, immigrants, disabled people, gay people – because no one should be ignored. All of these groups were connected with each other and with the rest of the city. He saw the struggles of all minorities as the same struggle.

"Rights are won only by those who make their voices heard."

What Happened in Miami?

In 1977, the Dade County Commission in Miami, Florida, US, joined more than 30 other cities across North America to make it illegal to discriminate against someone based on their sexual orientation. But Anita Bryant started a campaign and, in Dade County, succeeded in getting this anti-discrimination law thrown out again.

FIGHTING FOR ALL

Milk was a dedicated Supervisor and fought to improve the lives of everyone, not just the gay community. He called for better childcare to help support families and introduced a 'pooper scooper' bill to make dog owners clean up after their pets. He also worked to improve the public transport system, highlighting its importance by riding the bus to City Hall every day instead of owning or driving a car.

In 2019, 64 years after Milk was discharged from the Navy, work began on the USNS *Harvey Milk*, a giant US Navy ship named in his honour.

Want to hear more about someone who became a symbol of a movement? Visit page 54

Want to hear more about how laws can help human rights? Visit page 46

Want to hear more a public figure who was assassinated? Visit page 10

MAKING PROGRESS

When Milk introduced a gay rights bill for San Francisco in March 1978, 10 of the supervisors voted in favour – a major achievement. Only Supervisor Dan White voted against. Milk's bill became law on 11 April 1978. Then, on 7 November, Proposition 6 (the initiative to ban gays and lesbians from working in California's public schools) was defeated.

> "If a bullet should enter my brain, let that bullet destroy every closet door." *

Dan White, the dissenting Supervisor, was a Vietnam War veteran, ex-policeman and firefighter. Described as 'an all-American boy', he saw himself as standing up for traditional home, family and religious life. Homosexuality didn't fit with his idea of a decent America.

On 27 November, White climbed into City Hall through a window to avoid the newly installed metal detectors and shot dead Harvey Milk and gay rights supporter Mayor George Moscone.

The city was shocked and saddened, but sorrow turned to anger when, on 21 May 1979, White was convicted of voluntary manslaughter instead of murder. The existing conflict between the gay community and the police department exploded into what became known as the White Night Riots. City Hall was vandalised, police cars were set on fire and police attacked the crowd. In the end, White was only in jail for five years, but the death of Harvey Milk and the White Night Riots became powerful symbols in the continuing fight for gay rights.

*From a tape recording Milk made in 1977, that was to be shared if he was ever assassinated.

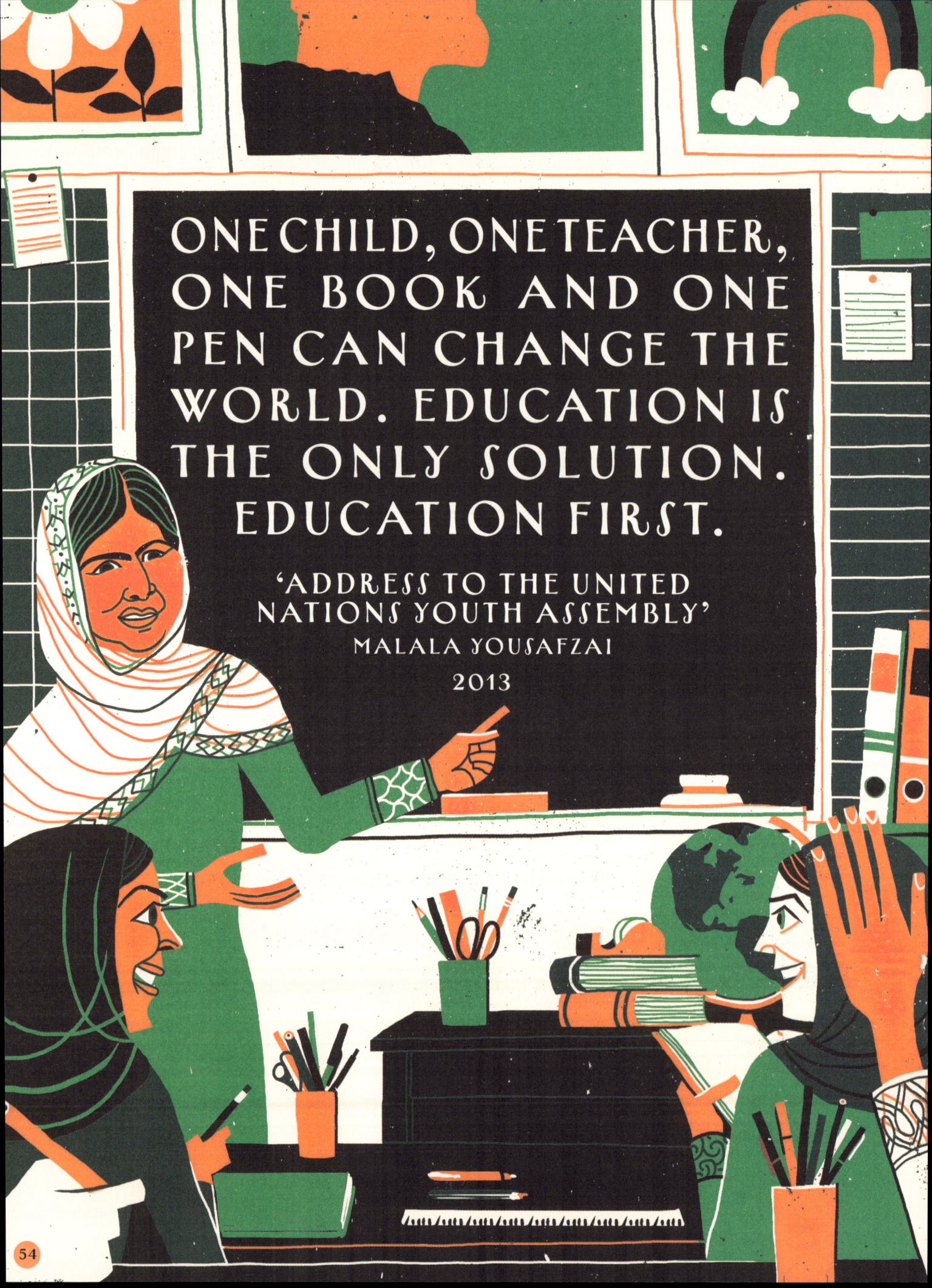

> ONE CHILD, ONE TEACHER, ONE BOOK AND ONE PEN CAN CHANGE THE WORLD. EDUCATION IS THE ONLY SOLUTION. EDUCATION FIRST.
>
> 'ADDRESS TO THE UNITED NATIONS YOUTH ASSEMBLY'
> MALALA YOUSAFZAI
> 2013

On 12 July 1997, Malala Yousafzai was born in the Swat Valley, in northern Pakistan. She was named after a famous female Afghan poet and warrior.

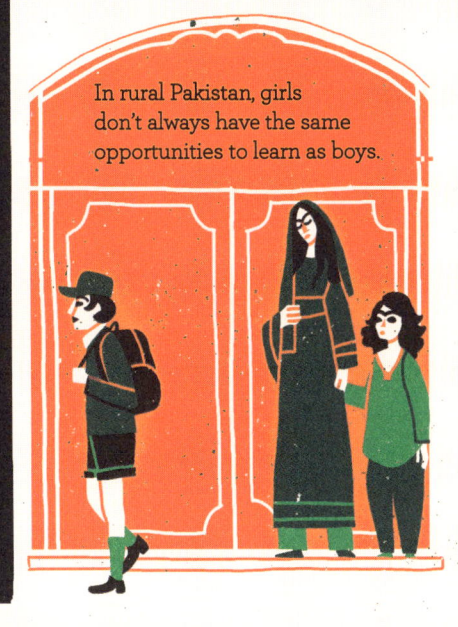

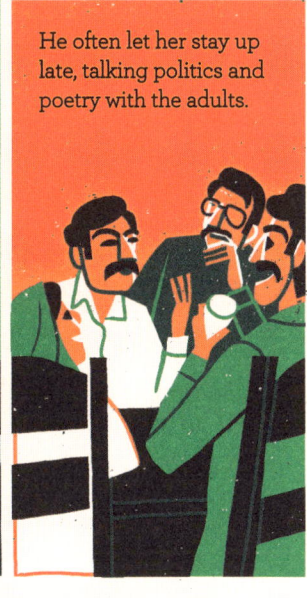

Malalai of Maiwand

In rural Pakistan, girls don't always have the same opportunities to learn as boys.

But Malala's father, a teacher, had set up a local school where both boys and girls could attend. He was determined that his daughter would have an education.

He often let her stay up late, talking politics and poetry with the adults.

Then, in 2008, when Malala was 11 years old, a violent group called the Taliban took control of the Swat Valley. The Taliban tried to force everyone to follow their extremist beliefs.

DIR
SWAT
SHANGLA
BUNER

The Taliban enforced strict laws and severe punishments, sometimes killing and torturing people who did not obey their rules. They had controlled the neighbouring country of Afghanistan from 1996 until 2001, when it was overthrown by United States and UK forces. Afterwards, they regrouped and rearmed in Pakistan and began taking over the Swat Valley where Malala lived.

Their rules meant television, music and films were banned; women were forced to cover their bodies and faces; and girls were forbidden from going to school. Malala wanted to stay in school but it was too dangerous. What could she do?

Encouraged by her father, Malala started writing a blog for the BBC, so that people around the world could learn what was happening in Taliban-controlled areas. She used the pen name 'Gul Makai' (meaning 'cornflower' in Urdu, the language of Pakistan).

On 8 February 2009, Malala wrote: "I felt hurt on opening my wardrobe and seeing my uniform, school bag and geometry box. Boys' schools are opening tomorrow. But the Taliban have banned girls' education."

Malala wrote her blog in secret, but with the support of her family and spurred on by her messages reaching a worldwide audience, she also appeared in public. Appearing on local and international television and film, Malala defended girls' rights to learn. In 2011, Malala was nominated for the International Children's Peace Prize.

Malala's campaigning, however, angered the Taliban, who did not like opposition. They resorted to greater acts of brutality and terrorism in order to enforce their rules. Malala and her father had become two of their main targets.

55

On 9 October 2012, Malala was attacked.

A gunman boarded the bus that she and her friends were on. "Who is Malala?" he asked. When her friends looked towards her, he raised his gun and fired.

A single bullet injured Malala in the head, neck and shoulder, but, miraculously, she survived. She was taken to a Pakistani hospital and then flown to the UK for surgery.

It wasn't safe for the Yousafzai family to return to Pakistan, so they stayed in the UK, where Malala recovered and went to a new school. She said, "What I went through in my life was a horrible incident, but here [in the UK] the love of people really strengthened me. And it continues to strengthen me". So does her Muslim faith – she believes that Islam is about equality, which is at the heart of her campaign.

In 2017, Malala accepted an offer to study Philosophy, Politics and Economics at the University of Oxford.

Want to hear more about education for girls? Visit page 30

Want to hear more about the importance of literacy for all? Visit page 34

Want to hear more about young people speaking out? Visit page 66

MALALA'S PEACE AND JUSTICE AWARDS 2011–2017

2011 Pakistan's National Youth Peace Prize

2013 European Parliament's Sakharov Prize for Freedom of Thought

2014 US Liberty Medal (youngest recipient to date)

2014 Nobel Peace Prize (youngest recipient to date)

2017 United Nations Messenger of Peace

'ADDRESS TO THE UNITED NATIONS YOUTH ASSEMBLY'
12 JULY 2013

On 12 July 2013, her sixteenth birthday and less than a year after the shooting, Malala Yousafzai appeared in public once again to give a speech at the United Nations Youth Assembly in New York City, USA.

Thousands of people have been killed by the terrorists and millions have been injured. I am just one of them. So here I stand, one girl among many. I speak not for myself, but so those without a voice can be heard …

Dear sisters and brothers, we realise the importance of light when we see darkness. We realise the importance of our voice when we are silenced. In the same way, when we were in Swat, the north of Pakistan, we realised the importance of pens and books when we saw the guns …

So let us wage a global struggle against illiteracy, poverty and terrorism and let us pick up our books and our pens. They are our most powerful weapons.

One child, one teacher, one book and one pen can change the world.

Education is the only solution. Education first. Thank you.

Perhaps those late nights talking poetry with her parents influenced her speech writing – Malala used contrast, repetition and balance to full effect.

She also made use of warring language – "a global struggle", "powerful weapons" – turning the fight back on the people who had hurt her. For Malala, education will not just solve problems of illiteracy and poverty, but bring an end to extreme violence of the kind that she and so many others experienced in Pakistan.

The end of the speech drew on a famous saying by a nineteenth-century writer called Edward Bulwer-Lytton: "The pen is mightier than the sword". Malala used this idea to bring people together in peaceful action.

Despite her remarkable story and worldwide fame, Malala remained humble. She acknowledged that her speech was not about herself, but about the people and ideals she had come to represent.

EDUCATION FOR ALL

Later on in the day, United Nations Secretary-General Ban Ki-moon declared 12 July to be 'Malala Day', saying, "No child should have to die for going to school."

In Pakistan, a UN petition calling for the right to education was signed by two million people, and soon after the Right to Free and Compulsory Education Bill was passed. A government educational fund was set up in Malala's honour.

However, it wasn't the shooting alone that caused the world to sit up and listen. Malala's actions – her resilience and perseverance – were what won her the Nobel Peace Prize in 2014.

Malala has continued to campaign and fundraise for her goal. The Malala Fund, through which she fights for change, was established to ensure that girls around the world receive 'free, safe, quality education'.

WE HONOUR THOSE WHO WALKED SO WE COULD RUN. WE MUST RUN SO OUR CHILDREN SOAR.

'REMARKS BY THE PRESIDENT AT THE 50TH ANNIVERSARY OF THE SELMA TO MONTGOMERY MARCHES'
BARACK OBAMA
2015

Barack Obama was born in Hawaii in 1961. His mother was from Kansas, USA, and his father was from Kenya. He trained as a lawyer and worked in civil rights, before becoming a politician. In 2009, in an historic moment, he became the first African-American president of the United States.

In 1965, when Obama was still a little boy, civil rights activists attempted to march 87 kilometres from the town of Selma, in the southern state of Alabama, to the state capital, Montgomery, to demand that Black Americans be allowed to vote. There were three marches in total, known as the 'Selma to Montgomery Marches'.

Slavery was abolished in the US in 1865, but a century later, Black Americans were still facing discrimination, particularly in the southern states. A legal policy called 'separate but equal' forced Black Americans to use separate parks, schools and seats on public transport. In addition, a set of segregation laws called 'Jim Crow' laws denied equal access to housing, jobs, justice and the voting system.

In 1963, a young Baptist preacher called Martin Luther King Jr led a peaceful march to Washington, D.C., where he gave a speech to 250,000 supporters. It was a turning point in the civil rights movement, prompting the Civil Rights Act of 1964, which outlawed discrimination based on race, colour, religion, sex or national origin.

Throughout the 1950s and 1960s, Black Americans and their supporters campaigned for racial equality, which was known as the civil rights movement.

Even so, racism persisted. The governor of Alabama at the time, George Wallace, was pro-segregation. He made it compulsory for Black Americans to pass a literacy test before they voted, knowing many did not have access to education. Black Americans across the southern states protested against these unfair restrictions. Most protests were peaceful, but police often responded with violence. While taking part in a demonstration on 18 February 1965, an unarmed black man called Jimmie Lee Jackson was beaten and fatally shot by Alabama state troopers.

THE SELMA TO MONTGOMERY MARCHES, 1965

Bloody Sunday, 7 March

In response to the death of Jimmie Lee Jackson, 600 protesters set off from Selma – the hub of the voting rights campaign – for the city of Montgomery. White supremacist gangs and Alabama state troopers on horseback beat back marchers with whips and tear gas as they tried to cross the Edmund Pettus Bridge. The event was televised and the footage shocked many Americans.

Turnaround Tuesday, 9 March

Two days later, Martin Luther King Jr led a crowd of more than 2,000 across the bridge – but when state troopers once again blocked them on their path, King insisted they retreat to prevent anyone being hurt. That night, however, one of the activists, a white minister named James Reeb, was beaten and murdered by a white supremacist gang. This prompted national outcry.

The Third March, 21 March

Protesters tried again. This time, in response to nationwide pressure, the Alabama National Guard and US Army were sent in to protect those marching. Four days later, on 25 March, after walking 12 hours a day, they arrived in Montgomery. Nearly 50,000 supporters welcomed them. Their petition resulted in the Voting Rights Act, which became law on 6 August 1965, and prevented racial discrimination in voting.

59

50 YEARS ON FROM THE SELMA MARCHES

The 7 March 2015 was the 50th anniversary of Bloody Sunday. Six years into his presidency, Barack Obama gave a speech in front of the Edmund Pettus Bridge in Alabama to mark the occasion.

There are places, and moments in America where this nation's destiny has been decided …

Selma is such a place.

In one afternoon fifty years ago, so much of our turbulent history – the stain of slavery and anguish of civil war; the yoke of segregation and tyranny of Jim Crow; the death of four little girls in Birmingham; and the dream of a Baptist preacher – all that history met on this bridge …

Obama's account of the marches included big, global events but also the words of one man – the Baptist preacher, Martin Luther King Jr. By doing this, Obama showed that the Selma Bridge marches were part of a wider story of persecution, injustice and individual action. By locating his speech at the bridge, he created a personal connection between his audience and that history.

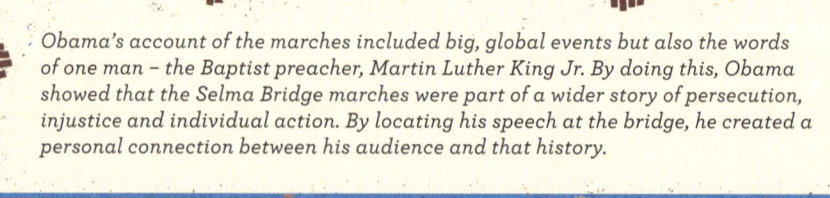

The Four Girls from Birmingham

On 15 September 1963, terrorist members of a white supremacist group called the Ku Klux Klan set off a dynamite bomb under the 16th Street Baptist Church in the town of Birmingham in Alabama, killing four girls. Despite worldwide outrage, it took decades to bring the men behind the attack to justice.

"Our march is not yet finished."

In his speech, Obama pointed to the continuing racial inequality and discrimination in parts of America's political system, institutions and society. His message at the Edmund Pettus Bridge was that Americans needed to work together towards a fairer society. "Because the single-most powerful word in our democracy is the word 'We.' 'We The People.' 'We Shall Overcome.' 'Yes We Can.' That word is owned by no one. It belongs to everyone."

The march on Selma was part of a broader campaign that spanned generations; the leaders that day [were] part of a long line of heroes.

We gather here to celebrate them. We gather here to honour the courage of ordinary Americans willing to endure billy clubs and the chastening rod; tear gas and the trampling hoof …

And it is you, the young and fearless at heart, the most diverse and educated generation in our history, who the nation is waiting to follow …

Fifty years from Bloody Sunday, our march is not yet finished, but we're getting closer. Our job's easier because someone already got us through that first mile. Somebody already got us over that bridge …

We honour those who walked so we could run. We must run so our children soar.

Obama's speeches were often modelled on those of Baptist preachers, like Martin Luther King Jr. "We gather here today" is a phrase associated with religious pastors. And like King, Obama's speech was passionate, poetic and contained biblical references. There is also a call for action – he urged the younger generations to take a leading role in an ongoing struggle for equality.

Here, Obama emphasised a need for building on the work of past individuals for future generations. His sentences themselves were crafted to do this – the second sentence continues from, and builds on, the message of the one before it.

THE NEXT STEPS

Obama said the actions of those marching from Selma to Montgomery in 1965 paved his way to the White House. It was inconceivable in the 1960s that a black person could hold the highest office in the country. Obama stressed the need to build always on the work of those who had taken the first steps in the civil rights movement.

Want to hear more about peaceful protests? Visit page 26

Want to hear more about citizenship? Visit page 18

Want to hear more about black history? Visit page 42

61

THE TASK IS SO IMMENSE AND THE ENDEAVOUR SO IMPORTANT THAT EVERY HELPING HAND IS NEEDED.

'STATEMENT TO THE WHO WORLD HEALTH ASSEMBLY IN GENEVA'
ANGELA MERKEL
2015

Angela Merkel was born in 1954 in West Germany but grew up in communist East Germany. Her parents encouraged her to be ambitious. Merkel studied physics and quantum chemistry and worked as a research scientist, before going into politics in 1990, when East and West Germany were reunified. Her career grew and, in 2005, she became Germany's first female chancellor (leader of the German government). As chancellor, Merkel has played a role in world politics and has been a driving force on global health.

THE EBOLA EPIDEMIC

In 2013, a rare, severe and highly contagious disease called Ebola broke out across West Africa, spreading from Guinea to Liberia and Sierra Leone and into pockets of other nearby countries. Between 2013 and 2016, over 28,000 people fell ill with the disease and more than 11,000 people died.

The disease caused huge disruption as medical centres filled up, schools had to close, and travel and trade were restricted. Ebola hit already impoverished (poor) communities, causing long-term effects on people's livelihoods and health.

Many experts criticised the World Health Organisation for failing to declare a public health emergency sooner and being too slow in getting money and medicine into the region.

The Ebola Virus

Ebola is named after a river in central Africa, which was the location of one of the first outbreaks in 1976. Since then, several strains of the virus have been identified. Today, viruses are no longer named after places, people or animals, but by their genetic makeup.

Zoonosis

Ebola is an example of a disease that humans can catch from animals. This is called 'zoonosis'. Scientists are still not sure exactly which animals carry the Ebola virus, but fruit bats are one known source.

WHO IS THE WHO?

The World Health Organisation (WHO) is an agency of the United Nations (UN), with headquarters in Geneva, Switzerland. Its members are a group of more than 150 countries who agree to work together to achieve 'the highest possible level of health' for everyone on the planet – no easy task!

The WHO was formed on 7 April 1948 – now celebrated as World Health Day. It has wide-ranging goals, including supporting universal access to good healthcare, monitoring public health risks, coordinating responses to global health emergencies and promoting healthy living and well-being around the world.

The Staff of Asclepius

The staff of Asclepius, the ancient Greek god of healing, with a snake coiling around it, is a symbol of medicine. For its logo, the WHO placed this symbol on the UN crest to signify its global approach to health.

WHAT IS THE WHA?

The biggest decisions of the WHO are taken at its annual meeting, when representatives from each member country come together in Geneva. This meeting is known as the World Health Assembly (WHA).

WORKING TOGETHER

In 2015, as the end of the Ebola epidemic was in sight, Angela Merkel gave an important speech at the WHA, urging all countries to keep working together.

Merkel was the German chancellor and also in charge of the G7, a powerful political group made up of seven of the world's major industrialised democracies (Canada, France, Germany, Italy, Japan, the UK and the United States).

Merkel's role in the G7 put her in an influential position in addressing other world leaders and decision-makers at the WHA.

'Statement to the WHO World Health Assembly in Geneva'

18 May 2015

In her speech, Merkel set out clearly to the World Health Assembly some key health goals of the G7. She wanted to encourage all countries, not just the G7, to work to achieve them – and their first goal was to learn from the Ebola epidemic.

There's an ancient proverb that says you should learn before you speak, and take care of yourself before you fall ill. Some words lose none of their wisdom even over thousands of years. Health is a human right …

Merkel opened her speech with an age-old familiar saying that reinforced the unequivocal fact that health is a human right. Enforcing this right is complicated, because inequalities exist in global health, with poorer countries less able to prevent their populations becoming sick and to treat them when they do. But this human right is vital for world health policy.

The disastrous outbreak of Ebola in West Africa made us painfully aware of how urgently the international community needs to act when crises strike … One lesson that we all need to learn is that we should have reacted sooner. We thus have to ask: how we can do that?

Merkel numbered her points: her speech was functional and factual. Here, she wanted to make clear that, in a globalised world, where everyone is linked through political, economic and cultural exchange, everyone's rights and responsibilities are interconnected.

Why are we doing this? Firstly, because the human right to health can only be enforced if a sustainable health system is in place or is put in place in every country on Earth, and secondly, because globalisation is tangibly making us all more dependent on one another, so that increasingly the health of one person is also the health of others …

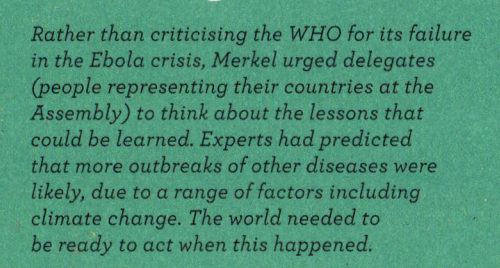

Rather than criticising the WHO for its failure in the Ebola crisis, Merkel urged delegates (people representing their countries at the Assembly) to think about the lessons that could be learned. Experts had predicted that more outbreaks of other diseases were likely, due to a range of factors including climate change. The world needed to be ready to act when this happened.

> We need some kind of global disaster response plan. And the World Health Organization must play a key part in this …

Merkel closed with an appeal and a commitment. 'Bargaining' is a clever device of persuasive speech – the speaker is more likely to get what they want if they offer something in return. Merkel wanted cooperation on the G7's goals as laid out in her speech, and promised that, in return, the G7 countries would help the WHO in its task of achieving sustainable global health for all.

> Every single person is vitally needed to fight for the human right to health … The task is so immense and the endeavour so important that every helping hand is needed. Therefore may I say a final sincere thank you for your efforts to help humankind … G7 countries will endeavour to support and advance your work.

LESSONS LEARNED

On 31 December 2019, a report was picked up by the WHO office in China detailing a cluster of cases of pneumonia from an 'unknown cause' in the city of Wuhan.

The cause was quickly identified as a new strain of a coronavirus, and was named COVID-19. This time, the WHO was quick to act. The virus, however, was quicker: cases were soon being reported all over the world. On 11 March 2020, the WHO declared COVID-19 a global pandemic.

Despite the rising case numbers and huge death toll, lessons learned from Ebola helped save lives. Better infrastructure had been put in place in many countries, so that when the new crisis hit, laboratories and health centres were better prepared. The WHO urged countries to take a 'whole society' approach, looking at the way people worked, travelled, communicated and interacted in order to control the new virus.

HELPING HANDS

Merkel's motivation and her message to the world highlight the value of working together as well as the importance of individual action. In 2015, she told the WHA that resolving big problems like global health needed governments and global agencies to work together – but that solving health crises in our world will also take "every helping hand".

Want to hear more about science and politics? Visit page 38

Want to hear more about human rights? Visit page 46

Want to hear more about learning lessons from history? Visit page 58

I AM FIGHTING FOR MY FUTURE ... I AM HERE TO SPEAK FOR ALL GENERATIONS TO COME.

'LISTEN TO THE CHILDREN'
SEVERN CULLIS-SUZUKI
1992

I WANT YOU TO PANIC.
I WANT YOU TO FEEL THE FEAR
I FEEL EVERY DAY. AND THEN
I WANT YOU TO ACT.

SEAS ARE RISING

MARCH NOW

PLANET OVER PROFIT

'OUR HOUSE IS ON FIRE'
GRETA THUNBERG
2019

Severn Cullis-Suzuki & Greta Thunberg: Youth Voices on the Environment

SEVERN CULLIS-SUZUKI

In 1992, when Severn Cullis-Suzuki was 12, she and three friends raised enough money, selling lemonade, to fly from Vancouver, Canada, to Rio de Janeiro, Brazil, for the Earth Summit. There, Cullis-Suzuki, representing what the group of friends called the Environmental Children's Organisation, spoke to world leaders about species extinction, pollution and ozone layer depletion.

THE EARTH SUMMIT

The Earth Summit was a round of important meetings held in Rio de Janeiro, Brazil, in June 1992 by the United Nations. It was an attempt to help governments rethink the way they should develop their countries in the hope of slowing down or stopping pollution and depletion of natural resources. Bringing together representatives from 172 countries and 2,400 organisations, the Earth Summit was celebrated as an historic moment for humanity.

WHAT HAPPENED AFTER RIO?

World leaders signed lots of agreements promising to cut down on toxic fumes, invest in public transport, investigate cleaner alternatives to fossil fuels and protect biodiversity. Unfortunately, they didn't keep all of their promises and didn't act to prevent climate change or invest as much as they could have in green energy, or forest and biodiversity protection.

THE GREENHOUSE EFFECT

During the day, heat from the Sun warms the Earth's surface. At night, the Earth cools as heat escapes back into space. Greenhouse gases, such as carbon dioxide and methane, help to trap some of this heat in the atmosphere – the same way a glass greenhouse traps warm air – and this helps to regulate the Earth's temperature and sustain life. But a build-up of greenhouse gases results in too much heat being trapped and the temperature of the planet increasing.

CLIMATE CHANGE

Climate change is when weather patterns change over long periods of time. It can be caused by natural events, such as changes in the Earth's orbit or erupting volcanoes. However, climate change over the last 200 years has been driven by human activities – such as burning fossil fuels and cutting down forests – that have caused a spike in greenhouse gas emissions.

BIODIVERSITY AND EXTINCTION

Humans rely on there being a wide variety of living organisms on Earth for food, water and breathable air. Biodiversity is the term to describe the many species of organisms on our planet and the ways they interact. It is natural for biodiversity to slowly change; new species evolve and others become extinct. Extinction happens naturally at a rate of one to five species every year and is an important part of biodiversity and the evolution of life on Earth. A mass extinction, however, is when vast numbers of species – around three quarters of the animals on the planet – are lost in a relatively short timespan (in geological terms, this means under 2.8 million years).

At two separate occasions, 26 years apart, two school-aged children, one from Canada and the other from Sweden, delivered speeches to audiences of important decision-makers. They expressed frustration at what humans were doing to harm our planet, and what they were not doing to protect it from harm.

A warmer planet means melting polar ice caps and mountain glaciers, rising sea levels, and changes in seasons and climates. This will result in weather conditions that humans will find unpredictable and extreme.

GRETA THUNBERG

In 2018, when Greta Thunberg was 15, she went on strike from school in Stockholm, Sweden, to demand action on climate change. Her strike prompted a global environmental movement called Fridays for Future. Thunberg spoke about global warming and the climate crisis at the United Nations Climate Change Conference the same year. In 2019, nearly three decades after Severn gave her speech at the Earth Summit, Thunberg spoke at the World Economic Forum Annual Meeting in Davos, Switzerland.

SCHOOL STRIKE FOR CLIMATE

THE SIXTH MASS EXTINCTION

There have been five mass extinctions on Earth, the last one occurring 65.5 million years ago when dinosaurs were wiped out. According to a growing number of scientists, a sixth mass extinction is now underway. This time, human population growth and activity, such as destruction of habitats, the wildlife trade, pollution and climate change, are to blame. At the current rates of species loss, up to half of all species could become extinct by 2050. The loss of biodiversity will have a severe impact on humans. At the Earth Summit, one of Cullis-Suzuki's pleas was for world leaders to stop species extinction.

THE WORLD ECONOMIC FORUM

The World Economic Forum is a non-governmental organisation (NGO), which was founded in 1971 in Switzerland. It is committed to 'improving the state of the world'. Every January, a winter conference known as the Annual Meeting is held at a mountain resort called Davos. The 3,000 or so invited speakers and audience members are world leaders, wealthy business people, and representatives from universities, civil society and the media.

WHAT HAPPENED AFTER DAVOS?

Formal political agreements are not usually made at the World Economic Forum. Thunberg's environmental message, however, was well covered by the media and she has continued to campaign for politicians to act to stop the climate crisis before it is too late.

'LISTEN TO THE CHILDREN'
11 June 1992

In Rio, Severn Cullis-Suzuki took to the podium at the United Nations Conference on Environment and Development – the Earth Summit – with a warning, and a plea, to world leaders.

I AM FIGHTING FOR MY FUTURE ...

I AM HERE TO SPEAK FOR ALL GENERATIONS TO COME ...

I AM HERE TO SPEAK FOR THE COUNTLESS ANIMALS DYING ACROSS THIS PLANET, BECAUSE THEY HAVE NOWHERE LEFT TO GO.

NOW WE HEAR OF ANIMALS AND PLANTS GOING EXTINCT EVERY DAY, VANISHING FOREVER.

IN MY LIFE, I HAVE DREAMT OF SEEING THE GREAT HERDS OF WILD ANIMALS, JUNGLES AND RAINFORESTS FULL OF BIRDS AND BUTTERFLIES, BUT NOW I WONDER IF THEY WILL EVEN EXIST FOR MY CHILDREN TO SEE.

DID YOU HAVE TO WORRY OF THESE THINGS WHEN YOU WERE MY AGE?

ALL THIS IS HAPPENING BEFORE OUR EYES AND YET WE ACT AS IF WE HAVE ALL THE TIME WE WANT AND ALL THE SOLUTIONS.

I'M ONLY A CHILD AND I DON'T HAVE ALL THE SOLUTIONS ... I WANT YOU TO REALISE, NEITHER DO YOU ...

YOU DON'T KNOW HOW TO BRING THE SALMON BACK UP A DEAD STREAM. YOU DON'T KNOW HOW TO BRING BACK AN ANIMAL, NOW EXTINCT. AND YOU CAN'T BRING BACK THE FORESTS THAT ONCE GREW WHERE THERE IS NOW A DESERT.

IF YOU DON'T KNOW HOW TO FIX IT, PLEASE STOP BREAKING IT ...

DO NOT FORGET WHY YOU ARE ATTENDING THESE CONFERENCES, WHO YOU'RE DOING THIS FOR. WE ARE YOUR OWN CHILDREN. YOU ARE DECIDING WHAT KIND OF WORLD WE ARE GROWING UP IN.

PARENTS SHOULD BE ABLE TO COMFORT THEIR CHILDREN BY SAYING, "EVERYTHING'S GOING TO BE ALRIGHT," "IT'S NOT THE END OF THE WORLD," AND "WE'RE DOING THE BEST WE CAN."

BUT I DON'T THINK YOU CAN SAY THAT TO US ANYMORE ...

YOU GROWN-UPS SAY YOU LOVE US. BUT I CHALLENGE YOU, PLEASE, MAKE YOUR ACTIONS REFLECT YOUR WORDS.

When Cullis-Suzuki and her friends started the Environmental Children's Organisation, it was because they were concerned about young people and future generations. In 2019, Thunberg kicked off the Fridays for Future movement, encouraging young people to strike from school to protest about the climate crisis. In just over 6 months, more than 2 million pupils in 135 countries were taking part.

Both speakers admitted fear. Cullis-Suzuki asked the audience if they were scared as children; Thunberg wanted them to be scared as adults.

In her full speech, Cullis-Suzuki repeated the phrase "I am only a child, but ..." several times. She and Thunberg didn't shy away from the fact that they are young people. Instead, they turned the tables to show that 'even' children understand what adults seem to dismiss.

'OUR HOUSE IS ON FIRE'
25 JANUARY 2019

At the World Economic Forum in Davos, Switzerland, Greta Thunberg demanded that world leaders listen to the scientists and begin treating climate change as a crisis.

OUR HOUSE IS ON FIRE.
I AM HERE TO SAY, OUR HOUSE IS ON FIRE.

ACCORDING TO THE [SCIENTIFIC EXPERTS], WE ARE LESS THAN 12 YEARS AWAY FROM NOT BEING ABLE TO UNDO OUR MISTAKES ...

WE CAN STILL FIX THIS. WE STILL HAVE EVERYTHING IN OUR OWN HANDS ...

SOLVING THE CLIMATE CRISIS IS THE GREATEST AND MOST COMPLEX CHALLENGE THAT HOMO SAPIENS HAVE EVER FACED. THE MAIN SOLUTION, HOWEVER, IS SO SIMPLE THAT EVEN A SMALL CHILD CAN UNDERSTAND IT. WE HAVE TO STOP OUR EMISSIONS OF GREENHOUSE GASES ...

YOU SAY NOTHING IN LIFE IS BLACK OR WHITE. BUT THAT IS A LIE. A VERY DANGEROUS LIE.

EITHER WE PREVENT 1.5 DEGREES CELSIUS OF WARMING OR WE DON'T ...

EITHER WE CHOOSE TO GO ON AS A CIVILISATION OR WE DON'T. THAT IS AS BLACK OR WHITE AS IT GETS ...

ADULTS KEEP SAYING: "WE OWE IT TO THE YOUNG PEOPLE TO GIVE THEM HOPE."

BUT I DON'T WANT YOUR HOPE. I DON'T WANT YOU TO BE HOPEFUL. I WANT YOU TO PANIC. I WANT YOU TO FEEL THE FEAR I FEEL EVERY DAY. AND THEN I WANT YOU TO ACT.

I WANT YOU TO ACT AS YOU WOULD IN A CRISIS. I WANT YOU TO ACT AS IF OUR HOUSE IS ON FIRE. BECAUSE IT IS.

Both speeches were a call to action. While Cullis-Suzuki urged adults to stop negative action, Thunberg urged them to begin positive action. Cullis-Suzuki was less sure of the solutions to the environmental problems, but Thunberg was adamant that humans had the solution.

Both speakers urged adults not merely to talk about change, but to demonstrate change. They showed that environmental issues like habitat protection and fossil fuel extraction are within human control – and that you can make a difference, no matter how young you are.

Want to hear more about actions, not words? Visit page 14

Want to hear more about youth action? Visit page 54

Want to hear more about global action? Visit page 62

GLOSSARY

Aboriginal reserves These were areas of land seized by the Australian government from the 1880s until the 1960s. Aboriginal peoples in Australia were uprooted from their traditional lands and moved on to these reserves to keep them separate from British colonists. This also allowed the British to take over Aboriginal land for their own farms.

Advocate Someone who publicly supports another person's views. They may also speak on behalf of another person or group of people who, for whatever reason, can't speak for themselves or aren't being heard by those in authority.

African American An American who has ancestors from Africa and whose ancestors were black.

Afrikaans A language of South Africa that derives from Dutch, developed by settlers known as Afrikaners.

Afrobeat A music style that combines African traditional music and American jazz, with lyrics that speak about political injustice. It was coined by Nigerian musician and activist Fela Kuti.

Allies or Allied Powers The countries (including Great Britain, Russia and the United States) that fought together against the Central Powers (Germany, Austria-Hungary and Turkey) in World War I or the Axis Powers (Germany, Italy and Japan) in World War II.

Apartheid A social and political system in South Africa that was created to categorise people into racial groups and keep these groups separate. It was introduced in 1948 by the white-run National Party, who enforced new laws designed to restrict the rights of 'non-white' people (Black, Asian and Indian people and people of mixed heritage, who made up the majority of the population). Following a long struggle, international pressure and political negotiations, apartheid officially ended in 1994. The social and economic divisions caused by apartheid continue.

Boycott When a person or group of people choose to avoid or stop dealing with a country or organisation as a protest against something they are doing. It can be as high level as a country stopping all international trade, or as individual as deciding not to buy a pair of shoes from a company that uses child labour.

Braille A written language for blind people, Braille uses a system of raised dots that can be read by touch. Braille books and documents are printed from the back of the page, so the dots are raised up and can be felt with your fingertips. The chart below is the Braille alphabet.

Have a go at writing your name in Braille.

British Empire All the colonies and other territories around the world ruled over by Britain. The British Empire began its expansion in the late sixteenth century. At the height of its power in 1922, it was the biggest empire the world had ever known and its territories included Australia, Canada, India and many parts of Africa.

Census A count or survey of a country's population, run by its government. It is a responsibility of national governments to have regular censuses (usually every 10 years) to not only count the number of people in the country, but to record where they live, their age, sex, what languages they speak and what their jobs are – information used to decide funding for public services like education and health care.

Civilian A member of the public who is not serving in the military or police force.

Civil Rights The rights all people have in a society, which are protected under the law within their country. These include the right to education, freedom of speech and religious freedom – things that should not be taken away from anyone because of the colour of their skin, beliefs, sex, class or who they choose to love.

Civil war A war that is fought between different groups of people living in the same country.

Colonialism When one power (usually a country) takes control of another territory and its people, usually by force. A colonist is someone who colonises or settles in the newly acquired land.

'Coming out' or 'coming out of the closet' To say publicly that your sexual orientation or gender identity is LGBTQ (lesbian, gay, bisexual, transgender or queer).

Commonwealth Short for the Commonwealth of Nations, the Commonwealth is a group of more than 50 countries that includes the UK, many countries formerly part of the British Empire, and some other countries, such as Mozambique, who were not directly under British control. Their aim is to maintain political and economic cooperation based on historical ties.

Confederacy Another word for an alliance. During the American Civil War, the Confederacy was an alliance of 11 southern states that withdrew from being part of the United States.

Consecrate To declare that something is sacred.

Convict Another word for a prisoner.

Cosmonaut The term used for astronauts who are trained by the Russian Space Agency. Cosmonaut means 'sailor of the universe', from the Greek words *cosmos* meaning 'universe' and *nautes* meaning 'sailor'. ('Astronaut' means 'sailor of the stars', from the Greek word *astron* meaning 'star'.)

The Declaration of Independence The declaration made by the Thirteen Colonies (a group of British colonies on the east coast of North America) on 4 July 1776, announcing that they were breaking away from British rule to become an independent nation. That nation would later become the United States of America.

Democracy A form of government where people freely elect (choose) who will lead and represent them.

Discrimination Treating people unfairly because of their skin colour, gender, religion, sexual orientation, age, disabilities or physical appearance.

Disenfranchised When a person or group of people is denied the right to vote..

Dock, The The area of a criminal courtroom where the defendant (the accused person) sits or stands during the trial.

East Germany and West Germany After World War II, Germany was divided into four parts, each controlled by different countries. In 1949, the regions controlled by France, the UK and the US joined together to become West Germany. The remaining region, under the control of the communist Soviet Union, became East Germany. They were divided by the Berlin Wall and remained separate until 1990.

Enigma Code The code created by the 'Enigma machine' – a device that was developed in Germany at the end of World War I to encode secret messages. It was used widely by the Nazi regime during World War II.

Epidemic and Pandemic An epidemic is an outbreak of a disease in a particular community or region. A pandemic is when an outbreak of a disease spreads over multiple regions or the whole world. The difference is not in how serious the disease is, but how far it has spread.

Fingerspelling A way for people with hearing and sight impairments to communicate by using their hands to represent letters and words. This is known as a 'manual alphabet' and there are a number of different ones. In the one Helen Keller learned, the 'speaker' makes the shapes of letters using one hand and they are felt by the 'listener' with their hand. The first word Keller learned – 'water' – is spelt like this:

French government-in-exile When the Nazis invaded France in 1940, French leaders, including Charles de Gaulle (a French general and government minister), left the country and went to London to carry on the fight from there.

Fossil fuels Substances, such as coal, natural gas and oil, that form over millions of years in the Earth's crust from dead plants and animals. Fossil fuels are burned as an energy source industry, which releases greenhouse gases. These gases stop some of the Sun's heat escaping back into space and increase the temperature of Earth's atmosphere, which damages the environment. Fossil fuels are finite and non-renewable, which means there is a limited amount of them, and they will take millions of years to be restored.

G7 An abbreviation meaning 'Group of Seven'. The G7 is a group of the seven most economically developed democracies (Canada, France, Germany, Italy, Japan, the UK and the US) and other European political representatives. Since 1976, G7 leaders have met regularly to discuss global economics and important global issues.

Green energy Energy that comes from natural sources, such as wind, water and sunlight. Unlike fossil fuels, green energy doesn't harm the environment by releasing pollution, because it doesn't need to be burned. This energy is renewable, which means it will never naturally run out.

Guerrilla warfare When small groups of armed civilians fight against a regular army using military tactics such as sabotage, ambush and raids.

Hallow Like 'consecrate', to declare something is sacred.

Homo sapiens The species to which all human beings belong.

Illiteracy Not being able to read or write.

Incarcerate To hold a person in prison.

Indigenous Like 'Aboriginal', a word to describe the descendants of the people considered to be the original inhabitants of a place, before other people, such as colonists, arrived.

'Jim Crow' Laws A set of laws in the American South that segregated and discriminated against people according to race. Jim Crow was not a real person, but the name of a racist stage act in mid-nineteenth century America. 'Jim Crow' became a derogatory term for black people and was adopted as the name of these laws in the late nineteenth century.

Ku Klux Klan (KKK) A white supremacist hate group that formed in the US at the end of the Civil War in 1865. It carried out acts of terror with the aim of preventing equal rights for black people who had been newly freed from slavery. Later, the KKK also targeted immigrants, Catholics, Jews and other groups who were not like them. It was active throughout the civil rights movement.

LGBTQ A way of identifying yourself as being lesbian, gay, bisexual, transgender or queer.

Militant

1. (noun) A person using, or trained to use, aggression to achieve a goal.

2. (adjective) Demonstrating a willingness to use aggression to achieve a goal.

NGO An abbreviation for 'non-governmental organisation'. NGOs often work for social, political or environmental causes and are independent from governments in their decision-making.

Nobel Peace Prize An international prize named after Alfred Nobel. Nobel (1833–1896) was a Swedish chemist and businessman who made much of his fortune from dynamite, which he invented in 1867. In his will, he left almost all of his wealth to set up five categories of prizes for excellence in different fields. One of these was the Nobel Peace Prize.

Nuclear holocaust The event of vast areas of the world being destroyed by nuclear bombs. If the Cold War had ended in an all-out exchange of nuclear weapons, millions of people would have died initially, and millions more from the after-effects, including radiation poisoning and starvation because of sunlight being blocked out and crops not being able to grow.

Ozone layer A layer of the Earth's atmosphere that contains high levels of Ozone (O3), a molecule made up of three oxygen atoms. In this layer, most of the harmful ultraviolet (UV) light rays from the Sun are absorbed, which helps to protect life. Too much UV light can cause sunburn, eye damage and skin cancer, and prevents normal growth in plants.

Pacifism Opposition to war, violence, fighting and weapons. It is also the refusal to use violence to achieve goals.

Partition The division of British India on 15 August 1947 into the four separate, independent states of India, Pakistan (which at the time included the territory that in 1971 became Bangladesh), Burma (now Myanmar) and Ceylon (now Sri Lanka).

Patriotism Love and support of your country.

Poorhouse Before there were social benefits, the poorhouse (also known as an almshouse or workhouse) was the last resort for people who were too old, disabled or poor to support themselves. Inmates were given a roof over their heads but were kept in harsh conditions and treated like prisoners. Poorhouses were first introduced in Britain in the seventeenth century, and they continued there and in the US into the early twentieth century.

Public office A position of authority to which a person is elected by the public, especially within the government.

Radar From **RA**dio **D**etection **A**nd **R**anging. A system that uses radio waves to find objects. It was used widely in World War II to locate aircraft and ships and is still in use today.

Reparations The compensation owed to cover the cost of damage or harm caused to others. In war, they are payments owed by the defeated side to other countries involved.

Sabotage To harm the equipment, infrastructure, weapons or strategic plans of a competitor or enemy with the intention of stopping them achieving their goals.

Score Another word for 20. In Lincoln's Gettysburg Address, "Four score and seven years" is 87 years.

Segregation Dividing people by categories such as skin colour, religion or gender, and then doing everything possible to keep them separated from each other – separate schools, separate transport, separate living areas, separate beaches, separate restaurants and even separate toilets.

Self-government The government of a country by its own people, instead of being controlled by another country.

Slavery When a person owns another person and forces them to work and obey them. Slaves receive no wages for their work and their lives are controlled by their owners.

State troopers In the US, the police force run at the state (regional) rather than national (country-wide) level.

Strike When employees refuse to work as a way of persuading their employer to improve their conditions in some way.

Superpower A very powerful and influential nation.

Suffrage The right to vote for public officials and government in a democracy. Suffragists and suffragettes were women who campaigned for their right to vote in the nineteenth and early twentieth centuries.

Taxation A government system of raising money by charging people or companies a fee known as a 'tax'.

Terrorism The planned use of violence to frighten and intimidate people in order to achieve change. There are many different terrorist activities, such as public punishments, murder and bombing, as well as different motivations and different kinds of terrorists (from individuals to political regimes).

Treaty of Versailles The most significant peace agreement that helped to end World War I. It was signed on 28 June 1919 by Germany, its supporters and its wartime enemies at the Palace of Versailles in Paris, France.

ABOUT THE AUTHORS

JOAN HAIG

Joan Haig grew up in Zambia and Vanuatu and now lives in Scotland, where she is a lecturer and writer. In 2020 Joan edited *Stay at Home: Poems and Prose for Children Living in Lockdown*. Her debut novel, *Tiger Skin Rug*, was nominated for the Carnegie Medal. Mrs Chamberlain was her teacher.

JOAN LENNON

Part Scottish, part Canadian, Joan Lennon is a novelist, poet and non-fiction writer, living in the Kingdom of Fife, Scotland, at the top of a tall house with a fine view of the River Tay. Her historical novels for 8 to 12-year-olds include *The Wickit Chronicles*, *The Slightly Jones Mysteries* and *Silver Skin*.

ABOUT THE ILLUSTRATOR

ANDRÉ DUCCI

André Ducci is a Brazilian comic artist based in Italy. He is the author of two books, *Fim do Mundo* and *Grande*, published in Brazil and Europe. His works are distinguished by tropical landscapes, scientific illustrations and social themes.

SOURCE NOTES

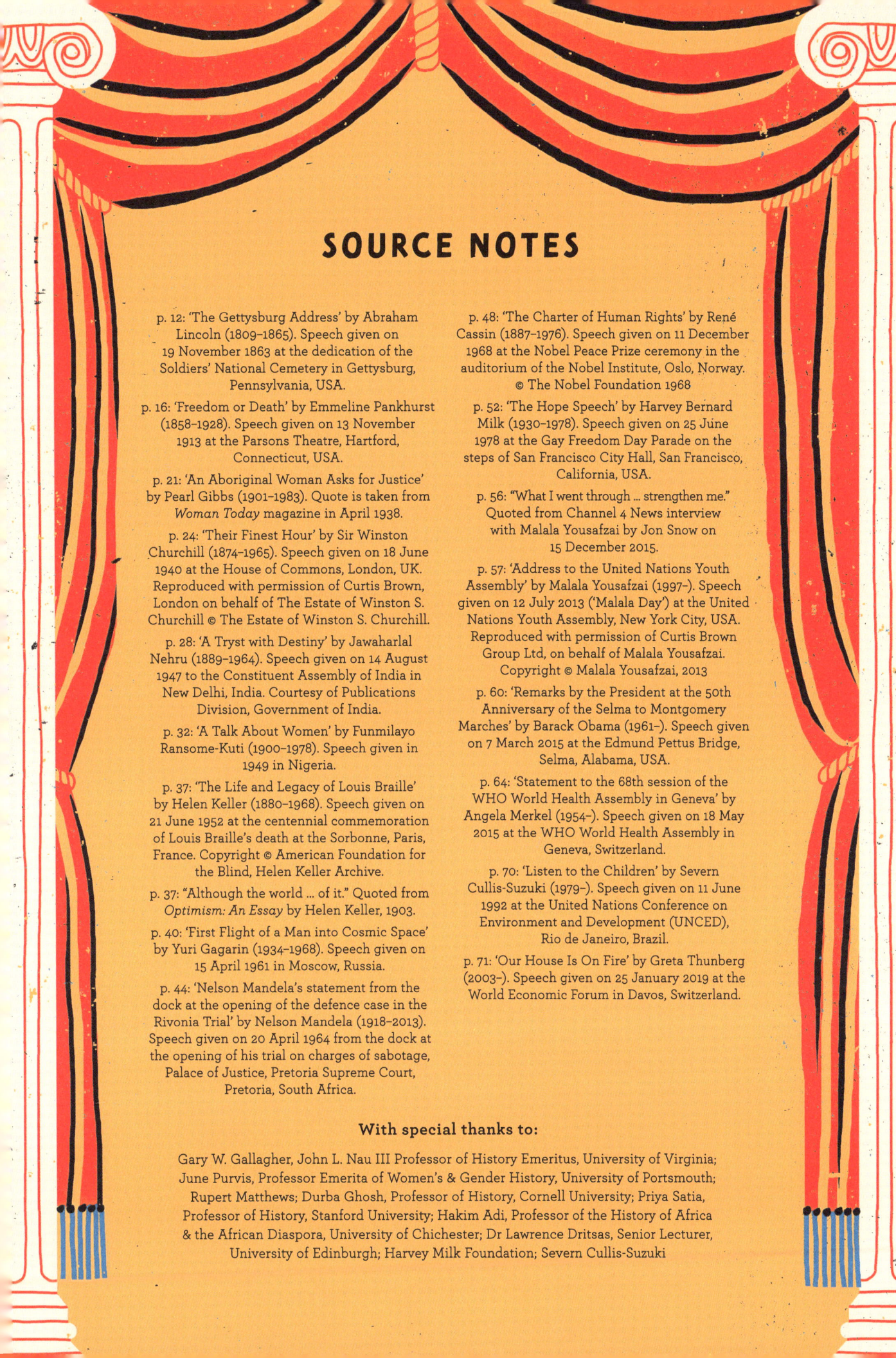

p. 12: 'The Gettysburg Address' by Abraham Lincoln (1809–1865). Speech given on 19 November 1863 at the dedication of the Soldiers' National Cemetery in Gettysburg, Pennsylvania, USA.

p. 16: 'Freedom or Death' by Emmeline Pankhurst (1858–1928). Speech given on 13 November 1913 at the Parsons Theatre, Hartford, Connecticut, USA.

p. 21: 'An Aboriginal Woman Asks for Justice' by Pearl Gibbs (1901–1983). Quote is taken from *Woman Today* magazine in April 1938.

p. 24: 'Their Finest Hour' by Sir Winston Churchill (1874–1965). Speech given on 18 June 1940 at the House of Commons, London, UK. Reproduced with permission of Curtis Brown, London on behalf of The Estate of Winston S. Churchill © The Estate of Winston S. Churchill.

p. 28: 'A Tryst with Destiny' by Jawaharlal Nehru (1889–1964). Speech given on 14 August 1947 to the Constituent Assembly of India in New Delhi, India. Courtesy of Publications Division, Government of India.

p. 32: 'A Talk About Women' by Funmilayo Ransome-Kuti (1900–1978). Speech given in 1949 in Nigeria.

p. 37: 'The Life and Legacy of Louis Braille' by Helen Keller (1880–1968). Speech given on 21 June 1952 at the centennial commemoration of Louis Braille's death at the Sorbonne, Paris, France. Copyright © American Foundation for the Blind, Helen Keller Archive.

p. 37: "Although the world … of it." Quoted from *Optimism: An Essay* by Helen Keller, 1903.

p. 40: 'First Flight of a Man into Cosmic Space' by Yuri Gagarin (1934–1968). Speech given on 15 April 1961 in Moscow, Russia.

p. 44: 'Nelson Mandela's statement from the dock at the opening of the defence case in the Rivonia Trial' by Nelson Mandela (1918–2013). Speech given on 20 April 1964 from the dock at the opening of his trial on charges of sabotage, Palace of Justice, Pretoria Supreme Court, Pretoria, South Africa.

p. 48: 'The Charter of Human Rights' by René Cassin (1887–1976). Speech given on 11 December 1968 at the Nobel Peace Prize ceremony in the auditorium of the Nobel Institute, Oslo, Norway. © The Nobel Foundation 1968

p. 52: 'The Hope Speech' by Harvey Bernard Milk (1930–1978). Speech given on 25 June 1978 at the Gay Freedom Day Parade on the steps of San Francisco City Hall, San Francisco, California, USA.

p. 56: "What I went through … strengthen me." Quoted from Channel 4 News interview with Malala Yousafzai by Jon Snow on 15 December 2015.

p. 57: 'Address to the United Nations Youth Assembly' by Malala Yousafzai (1997–). Speech given on 12 July 2013 ('Malala Day') at the United Nations Youth Assembly, New York City, USA. Reproduced with permission of Curtis Brown Group Ltd, on behalf of Malala Yousafzai. Copyright © Malala Yousafzai, 2013

p. 60: 'Remarks by the President at the 50th Anniversary of the Selma to Montgomery Marches' by Barack Obama (1961–). Speech given on 7 March 2015 at the Edmund Pettus Bridge, Selma, Alabama, USA.

p. 64: 'Statement to the 68th session of the WHO World Health Assembly in Geneva' by Angela Merkel (1954–). Speech given on 18 May 2015 at the WHO World Health Assembly in Geneva, Switzerland.

p. 70: 'Listen to the Children' by Severn Cullis-Suzuki (1979–). Speech given on 11 June 1992 at the United Nations Conference on Environment and Development (UNCED), Rio de Janeiro, Brazil.

p. 71: 'Our House Is On Fire' by Greta Thunberg (2003–). Speech given on 25 January 2019 at the World Economic Forum in Davos, Switzerland.

With special thanks to:

Gary W. Gallagher, John L. Nau III Professor of History Emeritus, University of Virginia; June Purvis, Professor Emerita of Women's & Gender History, University of Portsmouth; Rupert Matthews; Durba Ghosh, Professor of History, Cornell University; Priya Satia, Professor of History, Stanford University; Hakim Adi, Professor of the History of Africa & the African Diaspora, University of Chichester; Dr Lawrence Dritsas, Senior Lecturer, University of Edinburgh; Harvey Milk Foundation; Severn Cullis-Suzuki

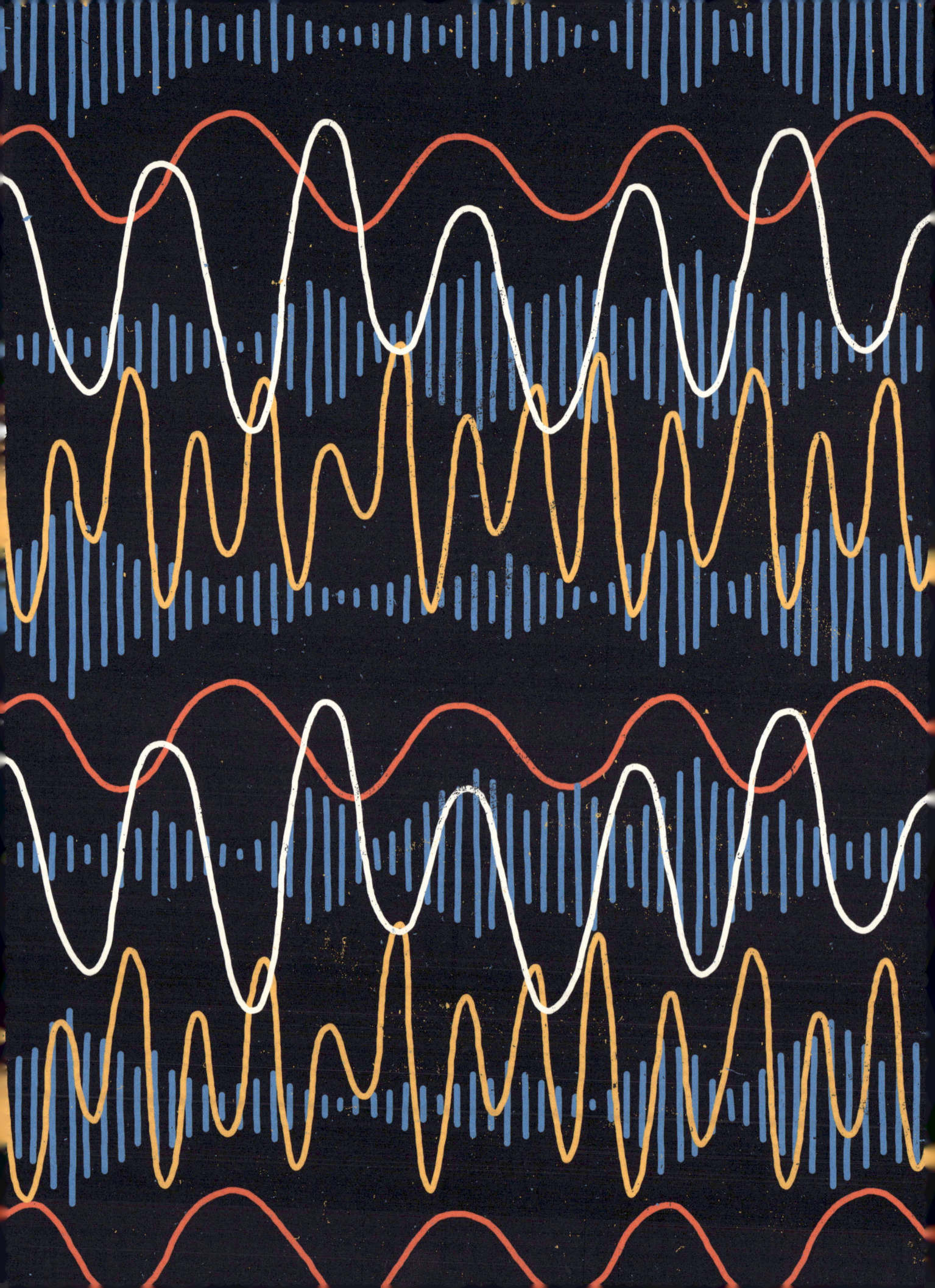